PSYCHO.COM

EILEEN ORMSBY

DARK
WEBS

For the Casefile fans
But especially for Casey McCaseface himself.

For the Casefile fans
But especially for Casey McCaseface himself.

PRAISE FOR EILEEN ORMSBY'S BOOKS

'Ormsby has delivered a triumph of narrative journalism, meticulously researched and gripping, a skilful mergence of tech jargon with human drama.' *The Saturday Paper*

'The book is a fascinating expose of this particular aspect of the "dark web" of internet dealings and its subsequent unravelling.' *Sydney Morning Herald*

'Ormsby's investigative journalism shines as she provides a very thorough account of Ulbricht's rise and fall.' *Penthouse Magazine*

'What pulls you through The Darkest Web isn't its often-nefarious, sometimes-gory details, but Ormsby's handling of three progressively intense narrative arcs.' *The Guardian*

'The darkness has become a repository for human cruelty, perversion and psychosis, and Ormsby captures all the tragedy in her gripping book.' *The Australian*

'A great strength of the meticulously researched Silk Road is the manner in which Ormsby gently takes the reader by the hand, unpacking the technology underpinning this 'dark net' market.' *Australian Police Journal*

'A disillusioned corporate lawyer turned writer from Australia, Eileen's new book, The Darkest Web, is the story of her journey, from drug markets and contract killing sites to the Internet's seediest alcoves. But the most startling moments of the book happen when she comes face-to-face with some of its key players.' *VICE*

'From the Internet's hidden drug dens to torture-porn websites, Ormsby has seen it all. If you've ever wondered what the Dark Web is really like, Darkest Web should be on your TBR.' *Bustle Magazine "The Best New True Crime Books You Can Read Right Now"*

'Riveting.' *Who Magazine*

'Investigative journalism that gallops along at a cracking pace.' *SMH Good Weekend*

'Through her clear rendering of the facts, Ormsby makes the intricacies of the technology involved accessible to even the most technophobic of readers. The tone is conversational and friendly while the content is intriguing and increasingly dark. In her quest to uncover the mystery behind the enigmatic DPR she uncovers a story of subterfuge, replete with conspiracy theories and hidden identities, that is rich with anecdotes.' *Newtown Review of Books*

ABOUT THE AUTHOR

Eileen Ormsby is a lawyer, author and freelance journalist based in Melbourne. Her first book, "Silk Road" was the world's first in-depth expose of the black markets that operate on the dark web. In "The Darkest Web", Eileen's gonzo-style investigations led her deep into the secretive corners of the dark web where drugs and weapons dealers, hackers, hitmen and worse ply their trade. Many of these dark web interactions turned into real-world relationships, entanglements, hack attempts on her computer and even death threats from the dark web's most successful hitman network.

Eileen started writing scripts for the Casefile True Crime Podcast in 2018 and has since become one of their most regular contributors. She often focuses on cases that have a dark web or internet aspect to them.

Twitter: @EileenOrmsby

ABOUT THE AUTHOR

Eileen Ormsby is a lawyer, author and freelance journalist based in Melbourne. Her first book, "Silk Road" was the world's first in-depth expose of the black markets that operate on the dark web. In "The Darkest Web", Eileen's gonzo-style investigations led her deep into the secretive corners of the dark web where drugs and weapons dealers, hackers, hitmen and worse ply their trade. Many of these dark web interactions turned into real-world relationships, entanglements, hack attempts on her computer and even death threats from the dark web's most successful hitman network.

Eileen started writing scripts for the Casefile True Crime Podcast in 2018 and has since become one of their most regular contributors. She often focuses on cases that have a dark web or internet aspect to them.

Twitter: @EileenOrmsby

BOOKS BY EILEEN ORMSBY

A Manual for Murder: FREE AND EXCLUSIVE

Psycho.com: serial killers on the internet

Murder on the Dark Web: true stories from the dark side of the internet

Stalkers: true tales of deadly obsessions

<u>Little Girls Lost: true tales of heinous crimes</u>

<u>Mishap or Murder? True tales of mysterious deaths and disappearances</u>

The Darkest Web

Silk Road

Keep going for sneak peeks of these books and to find out how to get your FREE TRUE CRIME BOOK

INTRODUCTION

Of all the criminals that walk the earth, none provoke such fear and loathing as the serial killer. Serial killers can't be reasoned or pleaded with, and one on the loose is the ultimate bogeyman. A news report of a serial killer roaming the streets stirs up fear and anxiety, even though the odds of us encountering one are tiny. Imagine, then, if such a monster could come off the streets into your living room, via your computer.

This new breed of serial killer may intrude on your life by way of a viral video; modern-day snuff, showing their crime in grisly detail, with a gruesome soundtrack to match. Perhaps they search for their prey online, lurking behind desirable photographs and agreeable dating profiles, waiting for the perfect victim to match with them. Or imagine a dystopia where a serial killer pops up as a YouTube star, with a following and fan base that places him squarely in "Influencer" territory.

You will meet these exact psychopaths in this book. All three stretch the boundaries of what we think of as serial killers, as their crimes and motives don't accord to any of the popular tropes we are so used to seeing played out on TV. They may not be household names like Jack the Ripper, Ed Kemper, or Ted Bundy, but they provide a fascinating glimpse into a new breed of killer with a very modern hunting ground.

~

Never in history have we had so much information on serial killers at our fingertips. Entering the name of even the most obscure killer into an online search engine will bring up a treasure trove of references; often a Wikipedia page, or perhaps an entry into Wiki's macabre cousin, Murderpedia. We can piece together a story from news clips and blogs freely available online. We can read about them in a book, many of which promise untold stories from victims who narrowly managed to escape, or provide insights from the killer's own family, friends, or colleagues. We can watch them in films or TV series, opting for the documentary or the dramatization of their lives as our mood dictates. Or we can listen to the tales of cruel tortures, peculiar rituals, and nightmarish victim ordeals while on our morning walk or doing the housework, thanks to the technology that delivers podcasts and audiobooks straight to our phone.

Our fascination with serial killers is boundless. They tantalize us, even as they terrify us. Although the term "serial killer" has been around for less than fifty years, salacious interest in such beings is at least as old as Jack the Ripper, and probably even older. Serial killers have been identified as far back as Ancient Roman times, hundreds of years BC.

According to Professor Mike Aamodt, who has compiled the most complete database of serial killers in the English language, we reached peak serial killer in the 1980s and there has been a clear downward trend in the number of serial killers we can identify since then. The steady decline since might be attributed to advances in forensics and policing techniques, or it could just be that the killers have become better at hiding their tracks (and bodies). Maybe they are choosing victims who might not be missed by family and friends, or whose disappearances are unlikely to be linked to one another.

Just as we have access to a myriad of information about serial killers, so too the modern-day serial killer has access to information their predecessors could only dream of. With the help of the internet, they can study the most up-to-date methods law enforcement has for identifying and tracking them, learn from the mistakes of their predecessors, or take a masterclass in investigative techniques or DNA profiling.

Indeed, one of the killers in this book did just that, meticulously documenting everything he knew and outlining his cunning plan to thwart any investigations. As it turns out, he failed miserably and is perhaps one of the least successful serial killers of the century, but his downfall came thanks to another internet phenomenon – people who are connected and communicate their every last movement to each other constantly.

Online forums and chat rooms, e-commerce sites, social media platforms, and dating sites became the new hunting ground. Killers could target victims who meet their particular criteria by targeting the kinds of sites that demographic was likely to frequent.

It was a chat room for gay men that served as the

meeting place for the first known case of murder where the killer and victim met online. In January 1996, Chip Hemenway killed Jesse Unger after the two men got into an altercation over Unger's mistreatment of a 15-year-old boy. Hemenway shot Unger three times in the basement of his home while the boy watched. Afterwards, the killer again turned to the internet, this time to ask two friends to help him dispose of his victim's body.

Craigslist appears to have the dubious honor of being the most common starting point for many internet homicides, so much so that a Google search will bring up listicles of the most notorious so-called "Craigslist killers". One Washington Post article from 2016 claimed that no fewer than 101 murders had been linked to Craigslist. Jack Levin, a Northeastern University criminologist quoted in that article said: "Traditionally, the majority of murders were committed by killers who knew their victims. Thanks to the Internet generally and Craigslist in particular, stranger homicides have been on the increase."

The obvious place on Craigslist to find potential victims is in the personals section. Newlyweds Elytte and Miranda Barbour lured 42-year-old Troy LaFerrara to his death with an ad promising a young girl's "companionship" in return for $100. When he arrived for the encounter, the teenage Miranda told him she was only 16 and asked if he still wanted to go ahead. She claimed that she would have let him go had he done the right thing, but LaFerrara wanted to proceed with the transaction, so she stabbed him while her 22-year-old husband of three weeks hid in the back seat of the car. Miranda Barbour later claimed to be a serial killer targeting men who paid underage women for sex, but there was no evidence this was true.

In 2009, 23-year-old medical student Philip Markoff attacked and robbed three women he met through their advertisements of erotic services. He murdered one of the women, Julissa Brisman, earning him the first known use of the term "Craigslist Killer" in the press.

In some circumstances, the killer would post a phony job advertisement to lure a person of a particular demographic to the murderer's house. Thus in 2007, Michael John Anderson, posing as a woman, posted an ad looking for a babysitter in order to lure young women. He killed 24-year-old Katherine Ann Olson, who applied for the position.

Richard Beasley, also known as "Chaplain Rich," lured three men to their deaths using a Craigslist ad for a nonexistent job in 2011. Chaplain Rich was a wanted man and needed at least one new identity, as well as cash to enable him to evade the authorities. He was able to word the advertisement to attract middle-aged white men similar to himself, and then ascertain they were not likely to be missed with a carefully worded questionnaire before he offered them the position.

Hand-in-hand with the internet came the smartphone. With half the world's population walking around with a camera in their pocket, there is more chance than ever before of capturing death and mayhem on film. Publishing it to the world takes a matter of seconds. This meant that deaths - both accidental and deliberate - were being digitally captured, bringing the long-held myth of snuff films closer than ever to becoming reality.

Snuff films are difficult to categorize, but the generally accepted meaning seems to be murder on film for commercial gain. It's a bit like the Stewart's test for obscenity: you may not know how to define it, but you know it when you see it. However, despite the snuff film being a ubiquitous staple of popular culture, prior to this century, there had never been a single verified example of a snuff movie. It is one of those myths that people cling to ferociously, reasoning that humans are capable of all kinds of depravity – it *could* happen, so it *must* happen.

The internet-plus-phone combination meant that more deaths than ever before were caught on film and uploaded to an instant audience. Terrorists, particularly the Islamic State, began deliberately filming and circulating beheadings as warnings to those ideologically opposed to them and their message. Drug cartels similarly filmed the torture and murder of rival gang members and their families and posted them online as a warning to others.

The most shocking example came in March 2019 when a white supremacist carried out a mass shooting in Christchurch, New Zealand, killing 51 people in two mosques. The perpetrator carried a video camera and live-streamed his murderous rampage directly to Facebook, where it soon attracted hundreds of viewers who egged him on in real time. Viewers copied it and shared it on other social media platforms, including YouTube, LiveLeak, and Twitter. Despite efforts to contain it, the clip has been seen by millions of people.

None of these pieces of internet footage are generally considered 'snuff'. Two films that closely resemble the snuff definition share similar names. *1 Lunatic, 1 Icepick* depicts the murder and dismemberment of student Jun Lin by Luka Magnotta. That clip's name was an homage to one of the most notorious films ever uploaded to the internet outside the dark web. The 8-minute video *3 Guys 1 Hammer* is considered the litmus test for a viewer's stomach for gore. It has been downloaded and viewed millions of times. Most of those who watch it are in it for the shock value and never think too carefully about the story behind it. *3 Guys 1 Hammer* is the basis of the first story in this book - the story of the Dnepropetrovsk Maniacs, a pair of teens who went on an unthinkable murderous rampage which they filmed for the internet.

Serial killers have entered popular culture so firmly that specialty stores sell serial killer action figures, and serial killer tours take enthusiasts on morbid excursions to sites where acts of mayhem and torture were carried out. Despite their heinous crimes, some killers gain followers and supporters, with strangers writing to them in prison, offering to be penpals, friends, and in some cases, to marry them. This is especially true when the killer exhibits a certain amount of charm and their victims are seen as less sympathetic. The second story in this book, "Killer Petey", is an extreme example of a serial killer who became a bona fide celebrity. Killer Petey was compared to fictional characters The Punisher and Dexter, due to the perception that he was meting out justice to those who had wronged his family and to men who were guilty of heinous crimes.

Indeed, Dexter has a lot to answer for. The perpetrator in the final story of this book was obsessed with the fictional murderer to the point of trying to follow in his footsteps. He is probably the only person in history to write a screenplay detailing every step of his commencement into the world of serial killing.

According to Peter Vronsky in his book *Serial Killers: The Method and Madness of Monsters*, "Statistically speaking, identified serial killers usually turn out to be white males of above-average intelligence who begin killing in their twenties or thirties." None of the killers in this book fulfill the statistical profile in its entirety, but they all exhibit some of those characteristics.

This book is by no means an exhaustive list of serial killers who have somehow used the internet in their crimes, but rather a deep dive into the crimes, motivations, and psychology of three of them.

PART I

3 GUYS, 1 HAMMER

THE DNEPROPETROVSK MANIACS

Author's Note: the common spelling of the city now know as Dnipro is Dnipropetrovsk. However, the common spelling when referring to the perpetrators is Dnepropetrovsk Maniacs, therefore that is the spelling used in this book.

PART I

3 GUYS, 1 HAMMER

THE DNEPROPETROVSK MANIACS

Author's Note: the common spelling of the city now know as Dnipro is Dnipropetrovsk. However, the common spelling when referring to the perpetrators is Dnepropetrovsk Maniacs, therefore that is the spelling used in this book.

PART 1

3 GUYS, 1 HAMMER

THE DNIPROPETROVSK MANIACS

Author's Note: The familiar spelling of the city, more common as Dnipropetrovsk. However, for consistency and spelling, I refer... in the repertoires... Maniacs... the spelling used in this work.

A VIRAL VIDEO

In December 2008, veteran journalist Caitlin Moran was browsing the web when she came across a link on a chat board. The person who posted it had written: "See if you can keep your breakfast down after watching this! I couldn't!"

Such comments are common in the Internet age. We even have a term for them: clickbait. And so Ms Moran clicked, expecting something along the lines of an unflattering GIF of an obese person, or a gross food challenge.

Instead, Caitlin Moran found herself watching the beginning of eight minutes of footage that have entered into internet folklore. The video, entitled *3 Guys, 1 Hammer*, could be found on any of several sites with names like rotten.com, snuffx.com, and bestgore.com. These were the kinds of sites that encouraged members to scour the web and find the most graphic and disturbing images and films possible of murders, suicides, torture, mutilations, and accidents. The sites were competitive and tried to outdo each other with their depictions of real violence. They attracted millions of visitors, with the most graphic videos garnering hundreds of thousands of views and being shared widely among gore seekers.

In Caitlin Moran's words, the link: "took us to some footage shot on a mobile phone, in some bland, murky woodland. It appears to be early summer. Fifteen feet away there's a man on the ground. It's immediately clear that a great many terrible things have happened to him quite recently, and that he will die very, very soon." She watched one minute and 47 seconds of the video before turning it off, knowing she could not stomach any more. However, that short amount of time was etched into her memory, a horror that would never leave her.

Caitlin Moran wrote of the experience in *The Times* (UK):

A large part of me was working on the hopeful premise that it was a very convincing drama project by some students - the kind of thing that was about to become a big viral hit, and about which the Daily Mail would become enjoyably enraged.

Simultaneously, I was telling myself that it was probably a revenge attack - that this man had attacked a lover, killed a child, and although his murder was awful, in a world of almost infinite sorrow it was not the unconscionably profane insult to humanity that it first appeared to be. I was using the thought of torturous retribution as a comfort.

Neither hope was true. It was a real murder she had witnessed, and the story behind it was one of unimaginable horror.

HOOLIGAN ACTS

In 1988, in Dnepropetrovsk, the fourth-largest city in Ukraine, two baby boys were born. First came Viktor Saenko on March 1, and then less than two months later, on April 20, Igor Suprunyuk entered the world. Dnepropetrovsk was an industrial town in a country in turmoil as it struggled to adapt to its independence following the collapse of the Soviet Union. However, both Viktor and Igor were born into privilege or, at least, a comfortable middle-class life. Viktor's father was a computer engineer who worked with public prosecutions, and Igor's father was a pilot who spent several years ferrying around Ukraine's President Leonid Kuchma. Both boys had doting mothers and lacked nothing at a time when many of their fellow countrymen were queuing up at 6 a.m. for meager work rations and paying for groceries with coupons given in place of wages.

When Igor and Viktor met at school, each saw in the other a kindred spirit, and they became instant friends. Together with Viktor's lifelong friend Alexander Hanzha, they formed a trio that soon did everything together.

Alexander, the eldest of the boys by two weeks, did not have the same wealth as his friends. He lived in a poorer part of town where it was said that "rats the size of dogs" roamed the buildings. His father had passed away when he was a baby, leaving only his mother to provide for him. However, he had met Viktor in kindergarten, where shared interests in toys or wearing the same color shoes mattered more for friendship than economic status. Still, he did not have the same freedom or opportunities as the other two boys, and soon it was Igor and Viktor who became a tight duo, with Alexander joining them when he could.

The boys had an early encounter with the law when they were caught throwing stones at moving trains. When the police knocked on Viktor's door and demanded compensation for the damage caused, the Saenkos paid up and questioned their son about the incident. Upon learning that Igor was the instigator, they forbade Viktor from seeing him. However, Viktor didn't listen because he was infatuated with the peculiar and charismatic Igor, and his parents didn't enforce the prohibition.

Typical of young boys, none of them enjoyed attending school or doing their studies. However, Igor and Viktor had home computers – a rarity among their peers – and they spent many hours exploring the internet. As they grew into teenagers, they acquired mobile phones and began photographing and documenting everything they did, as teenagers often do. Igor's mother had returned to her job as a high-ranking employee of the district state administration, leaving him unsupervised for long periods.

During their time at the 96th Secondary School in Dnepropetrovsk, the three boys lived in fear of the older and stronger students who dominated the playground, inflicting cruel punishments on those they perceived as weak. Igor and Viktor shared a fear of heights, and they were concerned that it would attract the bullies' attention and result in severe consequences for their perceived weakness.

Eager to find answers to their questions, Igor searched the internet for advice on overcoming acrophobia. One site recommended confronting such fears head-on, and Igor convinced Viktor to spend hours standing on a balcony of a 14th-floor apartment, leaning over the railing and gazing straight down until their vertigo subsided and their fear of heights diminished. They considered the face-your-fears method a resounding success.

Instead of gaining empathy from their own experiences with bullies, Igor, Viktor, and Alexander grew increasingly aggressive and antisocial toward those they deemed weaker than them, targeting younger and smaller boys. In the eighth grade, Igor brutally assaulted another child and stole his bicycle, which he later gave to Viktor. Although he caught the attention of the police, he was not charged, and rumors circulated that this was due to his influential parents' intervention. Viktor's parents once again forbade him from being friends with Igor, but they didn't supervise him closely or question his whereabouts, so the two boys continued to see each other.

Later that year, Igor ended up in the hospital due to an incident involving glue-sniffing. In 2002, a teacher reported that Igor and Alexander had committed what was described as "hooligan acts" against her. Instead of facing charges, Igor was transferred to a neighboring school, and Alexander was sent to a vocational school. Local residents would later inform reporters that the trio terrorized the district during their time in school, but no one reported them to the police due to Igor's parents' influence, with his father seemingly capable of making any unpleasant issue disappear.

Ukraine failed to fulfill early expectations of becoming an affluent free-market democracy after the Soviet era, and the wealth gap between the privileged few and the majority was evident. While petty thieves stealing to support their families faced harsh consequences from a corrupt legal system, it seemed that those with wealth and connections could evade punishment for anything – perhaps even murder.

PSYCHOPATHS IN TRAINING

Warning: this chapter contains descriptions of animal cruelty

Separating the three boys and sending them to separate schools did nothing to dampen their friendship. As the dominant member of the trio, Igor began leading them into increasingly serious acts of vandalism and violence. He developed a fondness for Adolf Hitler and proudly proclaimed that he shared the Fuhrer's birthday. Igor enjoyed taking photos of himself with a drawn-on toothbrush mustache in front of the numerous swastikas he sprayed on any available surface.

Encouraged by the boys' success in overcoming their fear of heights, when Alexander admitted to a visceral aversion to blood, Igor suggested that they try the same method. According to Igor, the best way for Alexander to conquer his fear was to encounter large amounts of blood. Igor proposed capturing and dismembering the many stray dogs in the forest near Alexander's house.

And so, a new chapter began in the lives of the three teenagers. Capturing and slaughtering dogs and cats became a regular pastime. Soon, they progressed to torturing the animals before killing them. Cats were skinned alive, and dogs were hung from trees and disemboweled, allowing them to slowly bleed to death. Igor would then use the blood to paint swastikas on nearby trees or fences. They took photographs of themselves posing with the carcasses, amassing a collection of hundreds of pictures.

They continued this bloodthirsty activity long after Alexander overcame his initial squeamishness, and their actions grew increasingly cruel. They believed that torturing animals would toughen them up for adulthood. One day, they crafted a wooden cross and crucified a white kitten on it. They filled the kitten's mouth with glue to stifle its screams, taking turns shooting at it with pistols loaded with rubber bullets. They filmed the kitten's ordeal, laughing until it perished.

Meanwhile, the adults in their lives seemed oblivious to the activities the three teenagers engaged in when they weren't at school or home. Igor's parents led busy lives, occupied by their high-powered jobs, and his father was frequently away. Viktor's father also spent a great deal of time at work, but his mother was at home. Perhaps she thought the blood on his clothes was a result of normal teenage mischief, or maybe he was skilled at concealing the stains. Alexander's mother believed he was incapable of harming any living thing and showered him with attention. Discipline and consequences were absent from the lives of these teenagers.

In 2005, when the trio were around 17 years old, they brutally attacked two 15-year-old boys. The history books provide no explanation as to why they chose those particular victims or whether their attack was motivated by anything other than pure sadism. What is known is that the trio mercilessly beat the smaller boys, leaving them bloodied and battered. The victims suffered from concussion, broken bones, and permanently disfigured faces.

The parents of the 15-year-olds attempted to press charges against Igor, Viktor, and Alexander, but once again, Igor's well-connected and influential father intervened. Using their age as an excuse, the police decided not to pursue charges, much to the anguish of the victims' families. The brutal trio escaped with little more than a stern reprimand from their parents.

After graduating from high school, Viktor enrolled parttime at the Dnepropetrovsk Iron and Steel Academy to study metallurgical technology and took on a job as a security guard. However, these pursuits paled in comparison to his fascination with the internet. He and Igor had discovered websites where they could watch gore videos on the computer, particularly those featuring real murders committed by drug cartel leaders or beheadings by extremist and terrorist groups.

Alexander drifted between odd jobs, briefly working as a pastry chef and a construction worker, but remained unemployed for most of the time. Igor's father bought him a green Daewoo car as a graduation gift, but Igor showed little urgency in finding employment. To appease his father's demands, Igor declared the Daewoo a taxicab and became an unlicensed taxi driver.

The taxi served as the perfect disguise for Igor, Viktor, and Alexander's new favorite pastime. They began robbing people, attacking strangers and stealing their phones, wallets, and jewelry. Often, they would pick up passengers in Igor's car, take them to secluded areas, rob them, and leave them stranded far from home. Unlike Alexander, Igor and Viktor didn't need the money as their parents were willing to provide them with whatever they desired. They engaged in these activities purely for the thrill.

Alexander later admitted feeling uneasy about his friends' actions and their reckless assaults on people. Fearing that they might accidentally kill someone, he claimed that he would no longer participate in their robberies after two armed incidents on March 1, 2007.

In early June, Igor and Viktor picked up a man and a woman in Igor's makeshift taxi with the intention of robbing them, as they had done countless times before. Unlike their usual nighttime operations, they chose to strike in broad daylight, away from their hometown. Worried that the couple had a clear view of their faces and Igor's car, which could potentially identify them, Igor and Viktor concluded that killing the couple was the logical next step.

Public records provide no specific details on whether Igor and Viktor carried out the act, discussed it beforehand, or who did what to whom. It remains unclear whether the couple died from the attack or were left to perish from their injuries. What is known is that the duo didn't find the idea of crossing the line from robbery to murder disturbing.

It excited them.

CROSSING THE LINE

When Natalia Ilchenko woke at around 4:30 am on 26 June 2007, she felt that something wasn't quite right. She had slept heavily after an enjoyable evening with her daughter, Yekaterina and Yekaterina's best friend, who had come over to share a meal and catch up on the news. A teacher at the local university, 33-year-old Yekaterina was a sociable and outgoing woman, who enjoyed sports and was friendly with everybody. Over a delicious dinner, the three women had a good time, laughing, talking and eating as Yekaterina regaled her friend with tales of her recent vacation in Turkey. At around 10:00 pm, Yekaterina offered to walk her friend the short distance home. They invited Natalia to accompany them, but she was tired and wanted to go to bed.

With a mother's instinct, Natalia rose and checked Yekaterina's room. Her bed had not been slept in, despite her assurances that dropping her friend home would only take a few minutes. With increasing uneasiness, Natalia ventured out into the mild morning to look for her daughter.

She had barely left her complex when she came across

three women gathered around something on the path, their voices raised in panic. Venturing down the path, Natalia Ilchenko came upon a scene she would never forget: a woman's body lay in a pool of blood, her hands up as if protecting herself from something; but as Natalia told reporters of the 2010 Chilean documentary, *Los maníacos del martillo* ("The Hammer Maniacs"): "There was no face, only parts of it." There was no doubt that the victim was Yekaterina.

Horrified in the face of every mother's worst nightmare, Natalia screamed to the women: "that is my daughter, call the police," and then collapsed to the ground, allowing the darkness to overwhelm her.

~

AFTER WALKING HER FRIEND HOME, Yekaterina had returned immediately. She was less than 100 meters from home when she came upon two young men standing to the side of the path, partially concealed by hanging tree branches. Her thoughts were probably on the cozy bed waiting for her mere minutes away when Igor Suprunyuk spun around and struck her in the side of the head with the hammer he had concealed in a plastic bag. The blow killed her instantly, but as she lay on the ground, Igor continued to hit her with the hammer until there was practically no face left at all.

Igor and Viktor had ventured out into the darkness with their usual intention of robbery and violence, with an emphasis on the latter. They stole her cell phone and ran away giggling into the night, excited by the mess they had caused with their yellow-handled hammer. The robbery was a bonus, but it wasn't the main goal of that night, as would soon become clear.

Igor, full of adrenaline wanted to do it again. Immediately. Not far away, 45-year-old homeless man Roman Tatarevich was sleeping off a drinking binge on a park bench right across the street from the local prosecutor's office. Thankfully for Roman, he probably never knew what happened when Igor set upon him, bringing the hammer down on him over and over again, until every bone in his face was crushed. The two boys left him there to be discovered by unsuspecting early morning walkers.

It is likely that there should have been three victims that night. Viktor Pertsev was attacked near his housing estate. He was fortunate that a woman from a nearby hair salon began shouting and frightened the attackers away, leaving the 58-year-old man in a pool of blood, but alive.

~

SIX DAYS LATER, on July 1, Igor and Viktor travelled around 25 kilometers to the nearby town of Novomoskovsk. There they found their next two victims, Yevgenia Grischenko and Nikolai Serchuk. Little is known about the murders, or the victims, other than they too were attacked with either a hammer or a heavy pipe and beaten so badly that their skulls split open. Apparently, during the murder of 15-year-old Grischenko, a passerby spooked Viktor as he was dragging the younger boy's body off the path, causing him to fall into the ravine, but the murderers were not spotted.

Five days after that, on July 6, the two young killers had their most prolific day yet, slaughtering three people. Viktor had spent the day and evening with his girlfriend and then had called Igor to come and pick him up. The two decided they would carry out a few robberies before bed to earn some extra money. The first victim for the night was Yegor

Nechvolod, a young man recently discharged from the army, who was returning from the club in the wee hours of the morning with several drinks under his belt. Yegor had made it almost inside his house when Igor attacked him from behind. Neighbors recall the blood-curdling screams of his mother when she found the bloodied corpse of her son on the doorstep.

Just around the corner from where the returned serviceman lived, night-time security guard Yelena Shram was walking home after finishing her shift early because she wasn't feeling well. Yelena was a hard-working single mother who walked the five blocks home from work regularly. She was almost home when she came upon the killers. Igor struck her with the hammer he had hidden under his shirt as soon as she was within striking range. As with other victims, Igor continued to hit her while she was on the ground. With the callousness that was becoming their trademark, Igor and Viktor took the clothes from the bag Yelena was carrying to clean the hammer of her blood. Later, Yelena's mother would say: "There was not a part of her that was not destroyed. When we arrived at the morgue, we could not recognize her." Tasked with the job of identifying the body, Yelena's sister had to rely on her clothes, hands, and hair.

Shortly after Yelena's murder, Valentina Hanzha, a mother of three who shared a surname with their friend Alexander (but was no relation) was the next victim. Valentina had been the sole caregiver for her disabled husband, who was now left to fend for himself.

One might think that with seven murders in less than two weeks in an area of little more than a million people, the authorities would be on high alert. But somehow, despite the similarities in the attacks, local police had not linked them. No warnings were issued to the people of the industrial district that a deranged killer was on the loose. There was nothing to tie the victims together - the only thing they had in common was they were in the wrong place at the wrong time. Igor and Viktor had retained the cowardice of their teens and deliberately targeted victims who were not likely to be able to defend themselves - the elderly, drunks, or women. Even then, they had taken the victims by surprise, never providing them with any opportunity to fight back or escape.

The next day Igor and Viktor added the youngest names yet to the list of vulnerable people who would become victims of their bloodlust.

VADIM'S NIGHTMARE

On July 7, 2007, 13-year-old Andrei Sidyuk and 14-year-old Vadim Lyakhov from Podgorodnoe, approximately 15 kilometers from Dnepropetrovsk, woke up extra early to go to the river and catch fresh fish as a treat for their mothers. The two young friends often went fishing together, usually accompanied by a third boy who wasn't allowed to join them on this particular trip. It was 3:00 am, still dark outside, and the other boy's mother was concerned for his safety. Andrei and Vadim, not subject to the same restrictions, set out on their bicycles with only their fishing rods.

As they pedaled along the familiar country road leading to the Samara River, where they intended to catch dinner, a foreign car passed them. The green Daewoo taxi stopped a short distance ahead, and its occupants got out, standing to the side of the dark road with their backs to the approaching boys. Andrei and Vadim continued pedaling frantically, with no option but to keep going straight unless they wanted to turn back, which they didn't have time to consider before reaching the car.

As the teenagers neared the ominous figures standing by the road, both strangers turned and swung heavy pipes filled with sand at them, knocking them off their bikes. Andrei was immediately knocked unconscious, but 14-year-old Vadim managed to quickly get up and started running. As one assailant approached the unconscious child, he screamed at his friend to ensure the other boy didn't get away. Like something out of a horror movie, Vadim heard the fake taxi roar to life and start to bear down on him as he ran back down the road faster than he had ever run before.

Vadim's intimate knowledge of the area that had been his home all his life served him well as he veered off into the bushland and found a hiding place. Despite being petrified, he managed to remain quiet as one of the attackers searched for him, driving slowly past the area where Vadim had left the road. He heard the car come to a stop, the door open, and the sound of footsteps. He wanted to scream in fear or cry out in pain, but instead, he cowered in silence among the bushes.

Unable to locate the runaway, Viktor returned to where Igor was repeatedly striking the other boy's face with the pipe, as the boy lay on the road beside his bike. Viktor urged Igor to leave the scene of the crime. Reluctantly, Igor delivered one final blow before joining Viktor in the car, and the fake taxi sped away into the early hours of the morning.

Once he was certain that the psychopaths had left, Vadim returned to check on his 13-year-old friend. Andrei lay in a pool of blood but was still breathing. He seemed to be attempting to say something, but the words were unintelligible. Vadim tried to stem some of the bleeding with his t-shirt and placed his jacket under Andrei's head for comfort before heading to a busier road in search of help. Cars whizzed by the frantic, blood-spattered teenager until someone finally stopped and agreed to take the boys to the hospital. Andrei had no chance of survival and was pronounced dead upon arrival.

Vadim remained in shock as doctors, nurses, and orderlies hurried about their tasks around him. He longed for his mother, unsure if anyone had gone to fetch her. The images of his friend wouldn't leave his mind, and the memory of being pursued through the bushes by a psychopath wielding a heavy metal pipe replayed relentlessly.

Finally, two police officers approached him. Vadim hoped everything would be okay now. He prayed they would inform him that they had apprehended the murderers and that he was safe. However, he was mistaken. At a time when adults should have been most concerned about the well-being of a young boy who had endured unimaginable horror, Vadim's nightmare had only just begun.

THE FIRST ARREST

Larisa Lyakhova was startled to hear a knock at the door at 5:00 am that morning. Her son Vadim had left a couple of hours earlier with his friend Andrei to catch fish, but there was no reason for him to knock if he had already returned. Larisa was looking forward to a good day since the date was considered particularly lucky – 07/07/07 – all sevens, the luckiest number there was. Hopefully, there would be fresh fish on the table for dinner too.

The sight of the local police officer on her doorstep sent a chill through Larisa, and their words turned that chill into a fist of despair. The officer told her that the boys had been attacked, possibly killed. He urged her to go straight to the hospital emergency room. Larisa's thoughts bordered on suicidal as she made her way to the hospital with her partner, Vadim's stepfather, only to arrive and be told that Vadim was not there, but had actually been taken away by the police.

When Larisa arrived at the police station and demanded to know where her son was, they told her not to worry, nobody was interrogating him, they were just talking. Vadim told her that when the police arrived at the hospital, they had not allowed him to call his mother before snatching him from the hospital to take him back to the station. When the traumatized teenager began to pass out in the back seat of the patrol car, a policeman allegedly poked him violently with his weapon to wake him up. She convinced them to let her take her son home.

They had not been home long when a patrol car full of police showed up and demanded Vadim return with them to the station on suspicion of murder. Ignoring Larisa's pleas to let her son recover from his ordeal, they took Vadim away again.

At the station, they grilled the terrified, injured boy incessantly about the death of Andrei, trying to trip him up in his answers. They threatened him with transfer to a notorious youth detention center if he didn't tell the truth. When his story didn't change, they told him he would be kept in a cell overnight. Neither his mother nor stepfather were allowed to comfort Vadim, nor were they allowed to accompany him while the police questioned him and, according to Vadim's mother, beat him.

Vadim stuck to his story that he was not a murderer, but a victim. He provided the police with descriptions of the two men who killed his friend and was finally released to his mother only after she threatened to go to the public prosecutor. She took the terrified boy home, where he was plagued by nightmares at night and could not be left alone during the day, afraid that the murderers would come for him. In addition to that, he was distressed by his treatment at the hands of the very people who were supposed to protect him and had little faith that they would catch the maniacs who attacked him and Andrei.

Now that there was an eyewitness and an angry mother

who wanted to see the assailants caught, the police finally started looking into similar crimes in the preceding weeks, searching for a link to the murder of young Andrei. Armed with sketches based on Vadim's description, the police intensified the hunt for a pair of serial killers, bringing in detectives from Kiev. Although no official announcement was made, the people of Dnepropetrovsk talked among themselves, and news soon spread that there were killers on the loose who murdered with impunity, preying on the weak and vulnerable. The locals dubbed them "the Dnepropetrovsk Maniacs."

THE DNEPROPETROVSK MANIACS

T he two men at the center of the hunt, Igor Suprunyuk and Viktor Saenko, went quiet for a few days, perhaps rattled that they had lost Vadim after giving chase. But their bloodlust and hubris had them on the hunt for another victim less than a week later.

On July 12, 2007, Igor and Viktor pulled over on the side of the road between Dnepropetrovsk and the village of Taroms'ke in their green unlicensed taxi. As they preferred, the tree-lined road was quiet, but they knew it would have traffic at some point. Their plan was to flag down a passing car and kill the occupant, provided it wasn't a big guy. They parked their car carefully, in case the person they pulled over caught wind of what was happening and tried to speed off dangerously. They didn't want anyone to hit and damage their getaway vehicle.

As they waited by the roadside for their next victim, Viktor balanced his phone on the roof of the car and set the video to record. The teenagers were part of the digital generation, and they had taken photographs to document many of their exploits. As Viktor experimented with lining up the perfect shot, they discussed how the next hour or two might unfold.

Igor said to Viktor, "We can stop a car just like that, and if it's a big guy, we tell him there's no problem and let him go, and if a small one comes out, we say 'welcome' with this!" He pulled out a yellow-handled hammer from a yellow plastic bag and brandished it at the camera as both he and Viktor laughed in excitement. Encouraged by his friend's approval, Igor played it up for the camera. He hid the hammer behind his back, then exclaimed, "I will pull it out like this!" and demonstrated the swinging motion that had already brought at least eight people to their demise.

They no longer even pretended that robbery was their main motive. The boys who had been on the road the previous week had nothing but their fishing rods with them, and as they discussed their plans for the day, there was no mention of targeting wealthier individuals. All they cared about was finding a target who would be unlikely or unable to fight back, as they were still cowards at heart. Their motive was the thrill of the kill, and they wanted to capture it all on camera to relive later.

The road was quieter than usual that day, and Igor and Viktor used the time to discuss the logistics of different people passing by. They had binoculars so they could see well into the distance and figure out if the approaching person was a suitable victim. They hoped that whoever it was had a cell phone, nice but not too nice, as they wanted to be able to sell it quickly. If it was a man and a woman, they would proceed to kill them both, provided the man wasn't too big.

While they waited, they inspected the car, noting the stains in various spots that were undoubtedly blood from their previous victims. They chatted and argued about which stains came from which person, sounding like two ordinary, slightly bored young men waiting for roadside assistance.

Finally, Viktor raised the binoculars and saw someone coming down the quiet stretch of road. He called out to Igor that it was time. He exclaimed in excitement, "What a video we will capture! Not just pictures!"

"What does he look like?" Igor asked.

"He looks normal," Viktor responded.

3 GUYS, 1 HAMMER

Sergei Yatzenko had cheated death twice. Around 1990, while working on a farm, he lost control of the tractor he was driving, and it rolled into the river. He could have jumped out of the cabin before it hit the water, but instead, he tried to save the expensive farm machinery for its owner and ended up pinned underwater. By the time he was freed, Sergei was clinically dead from drowning. Rescuers managed to resuscitate him and get him to the hospital, where doctors declared his survival a one-in-a-million chance.

A young father at the time, Sergei went on to devote himself to his family. He had a wife, Ludmilla, who adored him, and two sons who grew up to be fine young men, and who married young women whom Sergei came to love as if they were his own daughters. Sergei worked hard to give his family everything they needed. He was a wonderful cook, a loving father, always cheerful, and met all of life's challenges with good humor. When a grandson came along, Sergei could not have been happier. He took it upon himself to teach his daughter-in-law how to swaddle and bathe the baby, which she indulged in the spirit in which it was offered. Sergei could not get enough of caring for and playing with his grandson and taking him for long walks.

Sergei's life had been dealt a second blow when he developed a cancerous tumor in his throat that needed emergency surgery. It was another life-and-death operation for Sergei, which he faced with strength and dignity. As Ludmilla said, "When the tumor was discovered, he did not complain, he did not whine, he took everything like a man." They were both overjoyed when the operation was success- ful, but he was left unable to speak in anything more than a whisper of a few words at a time. He lost his job, but, Ludmilla said, his family heard him, and that was what mattered.

People often spoke of Sergei's kindness and gentle nature, but he was also a proud man, and by this time, he was looking after his invalid mother as well as his wife and the four dogs that he had given a home to. He refused to sit at home and feel sorry for himself, so he accepted any odd job that people would give him. He was happy to take on building tasks, fixing cars, garbage collection, driving, or making deliveries on his Dnepr, a small Ukrainian-made off-road motorbike. According to Ludmilla, he even wove baskets and fashioned household goods out of macramé. His voice was slowly being restored, and he could speak whole sentences, though still in a whisper.

On the afternoon of July 12, 2007, 48-year-old Sergei called Ludmilla to let her know that he was going to get some fuel for his motorbike, and then he would go and see his grandson, just as he did whenever he had the chance. He set off along the lonely wooded shortcut to the highway. At some point, Sergei apparently swapped the motorbike for a bicycle. Perhaps he ran out of fuel before reaching his destination and left the motorbike at the side of the road. What happened here is unclear.

What we do know is that along that quiet stretch of road, Igor and Viktor waited for somebody - anybody weaker than the duo - to come along.

~

ONCE VIKTOR HAD IDENTIFIED the target, Igor stood nonchalantly in the middle of the road, forcing the bike to swerve around him. Viktor realized that the camera sitting on top of the car would not do the trick, so he grabbed hold of it to capture all the action on film.

As Sergei rode past on his mission to see his grandchild, Igor swung around, hammer still in the plastic bag, and knocked him off his bike. Giggling like children, the two raced to the groaning man on the ground, Igor to hit him again while urging Viktor to make sure everything was caught on camera.

Still laughing, they dragged the innocent man from the road into the woods. Igor hit him in the face again with the hammer, but Sergei seemed to still be trying to speak, even though the cancer had already cruelly taken that ability from him. Igor stopped for a moment and urged Viktor to listen to the sounds coming from Sergei and to train the camera in a close-up on his face. After listening to the gurgling for a full minute, they returned to taunting Sergei's efforts to speak as they carried out their attack, Igor with the hammer and Viktor with a screwdriver. Viktor stabbed the screwdriver into Sergei's eyes until he could see brain matter, then drove it over and over into the man's stomach.

As Sergei continued to try to breathe, his face no longer there, Igor and Viktor marveled that he managed to stay alive. For eight long minutes in that lonely wood, Sergei Yatzenko endured unimaginable suffering at the hands of two psychopaths, which they gleefully caught on camera, giggling with excitement the entire time. They broke his arms, hit him repeatedly in the face with a hammer, and attempted to eviscerate him in their frenzied attack.

Finally, satisfied that he was dead, Igor gave him one last taunt: "What a fucking day for you, huh?" he said.

Igor took his time wiping the hammer clean and putting it in the trunk, and then carefully washed his face and hair, asking his friend to check for spots where he had missed the blood. Running his fingers through his wet hair, Igor seemed invigorated by the atrocities he had just carried out, crying, "This time was awesome, yeah?"

Viktor responded, "I don't understand how he stayed alive. I had the screwdriver like this as I stabbed him." He demonstrated how he had held the weapon. "I could feel his brain."

Viktor was keen to flee the scene of the crime, but Igor insisted the pair should go back and immortalize the memory with a selfie. Once he finished washing, he demanded, "Alright, let's take a picture," and they returned to where the bloodied remains of a proud, brave family man lay to carry out the final indignity of photographing them-selves performing the Nazi salute above his corpse.

~

THAT EVENING, when Sergei had not returned home and his phone was not answering, Ludmilla took to the telephone and then to the streets to look for him. She called her daughter-in-law and found out he had never made it there. She asked everyone the couple knew if they had seen Sergei.

She knew something was not right because he would always let her know where he was and if he was going to be late.

Ludmilla was concerned that her gentle husband had had an accident or fallen ill, as he was inclined to take on too much and over-exert himself. She was frustrated and upset that Ukrainian regulations meant she could not file a missing persons report until he had been absent for 72 hours, even though she knew he had not simply gone off without telling her. Ludmilla did not sleep that night, and the next day she posted flyers and photographs of her husband all around the town and stopped everyone she came across, asking if they had seen him. Nobody had, but Ludmilla did not give up. She scoured the streets and enlisted help from family and friends until she fell asleep, exhausted.

A CITY GRIPPED IN FEAR

As Ludmilla searched high and low for Sergei, her husband's murderers continued on their spree. On July 14, the pair targeted 45-year-old Natalya Mamcharuk, knocking her off her scooter, then dragging her into the bushes, where they killed her with a hammer. Igor and Viktor were becoming bolder, and several people saw them and gave chase but were unable to catch them. Natalya's murder occurred just feet away from a young pair of street children, a brother and sister who were cowering inside the makeshift hut of rags and cardboard they had built nearby. The children were able to provide police with a clear description of the perpetrators, which matched that provided by young Vadim Lyakhov.

Rumors of a pair of psychopaths on the loose were now spreading throughout the city of Dnepropetrovsk. Late-night clubs and restaurants in the district and city outskirts were empty of customers, and tourists stayed away from the industrial center. Children were kept indoors, and the city was gripped by fear. The tension was exacerbated by the lack of news coverage and official information from the police.

Over the next few days, from July 14 to July 16, two muti-lated corpses were discovered every day. Each victim had been repeatedly struck in the face with a blunt object and many of them had been stabbed and eviscerated while lying on the ground. In most cases, the mutilation made it difficult to recognize the victims. It was evident to the townspeople that a serial killer was behind these attacks, but there was no discernible pattern among the victims. As experts pointed out, serial killers usually have a specific type of victim, but these individuals had nothing in common. They were simply a diverse group of people going about their daily lives, seemingly attacked at random.

Meanwhile, Dnepropetrovsk witnessed an unusually high number of funerals. Young Vadim was forbidden by his mother to attend the memorial service of his 13-year-old friend, Andrei Sidyuk, as he was still traumatized by his ordeal. However, he would later visit his friend's grave with the other boy's grandmother.

Unbeknownst to the mourners, many of the funerals had two unwelcome guests. Igor and Viktor would attend the services and gravesites of their victims to take selfies, seemingly unnoticed, giving the deceased individuals the finger as one final act of humiliation and disrespect.

On July 16, Ludmilla Yatzenko received a call informing her that a Dnepr motorcycle matching the description of her husband's bike had been found abandoned in a bush. The person who spotted it led Ludmilla and her sons to the location. Searching the area, the family who meant every-thing to each other discovered a decomposing corpse wearing Sergei's gray, neatly pressed trousers. Sergei

Yatzenko had cheated death twice, but he was no match for the Dnepropetrovsk Maniacs.

THE RAMPAGE CONTINUES

More murders followed in such rapid succession that there is little information available about individual victims in records or newspaper reports from the time. In one instance, an eight-month pregnant woman was slaughtered, and her fetus was ripped from the womb. The victims were always vulnerable - children or the elderly, disabled or intoxicated, destitute or weak. Igor and Viktor's cowardice as young teenagers persisted as they became psychopaths. They were still afraid of anyone bigger and stronger than themselves.

The task force established to find those responsible for the murders grew to encompass almost every law enforcement officer in the region. They knew they were looking for two young men, thanks to the eyewitness accounts, and they had been able to create accurate sketches from the information. Still, they kept this information out of the newspapers, both to avoid panic and in the hope that the suspects would not realize the police were onto them. This was despite Igor and Viktor knowing that they had been spotted several times and had even left some survivors when they were interrupted or frightened and ran away.

One such survivor was 70-year-old Lidia Mikrenischeva. She had been walking her three dogs near her home when she noticed what she thought were two good-looking young men taking photographs. She assumed they were looking at nearby real estate and didn't think much of it. As the path wound through bushes, secluded from any passersby, Igor struck her from behind. Lidia fell to the ground unconscious, and Igor and Viktor took turns repeatedly kicking her in the face, hoping to dislodge what they believed were gold crowns on her teeth. Viktor once again played the role of cameraman. Each vicious kick to the elderly lady was captured and preserved on video, possibly to be uploaded to their favorite gore site at a later date.

Lidia's dogs were barking loudly, which startled the attackers. They shot the dogs with rubber bullets, killing two and injuring the other, but fled before they could finish Lidia off. She suffered serious internal and external injuries; her jaw was shattered, and her face had to be reconstructed. She was traumatized and broken, having lost two of her furry companions, but she had escaped the clutches of the Dnepropetrovsk Maniacs.

The Ministry of Internal Affairs distributed police sketches and lists of stolen property to local pawnshops. They confirmed that there was indeed a murderous spree occurring in the district and it was being carried out by two otherwise ordinary-looking young men, but authorities seemed perplexed by the crimes, as if unsure of what to do. There was still no official statement to the press, and residents in the Industrial District, the main area where the crimes took place, heard rumors of madmen on the loose, attacking people at night, but lacked concrete information.

This only heightened the fear. Officials would later disclose that they had over two thousand police personnel dedicated to solving the crimes, while the general public remained unaware.

Meanwhile, young Vadim went to bed every night, staying awake as long as possible, knowing that when sleep overtook him, the images would haunt his dreams. Every night, he would pray that the murderers would be caught and imprisoned forever before sleep enveloped him, bringing along the nightmares.

CAPTURE

Igor and Viktor's reign of terror came to an abrupt end at the cash register of a pawnshop on July 23, 2007.

The official story of how they were caught was that Igor and Viktor visited the shop to sell a phone from one of their victims for an amount that equalled approximately $US20. When the shop clerk activated the phone, police intercepted the signal and rushed to the scene. Another story was that the shop assistant recognised the two men from the police sketches that had been circulated. Still another was that police had arrested a friend of the trio, who had provided police with their names in return for immunity from prosecution. It may have been a combination of all these things. Stories vary between news reports and information from the Ukrainian police was often conflicting and always secretive.

Igor and Viktor were arrested on the spot and police officers were immediately deployed to conduct searches on their homes, as well as that of Alexander. When police descended on Viktor's apartment, they were refused entry for a considerable time before Viktor's father finally let them in the house.

Police retrieved items from the wardrobes of the suspects and according to the investigator who bagged the clothes, there was not a single item from Igor and Viktor's belongings that were without bloodstains. The jeans, sneakers and jackets were all soiled in a varying intensity of red and brown. Among the evidence collected was the bloody earring ripped from the ear of one of their victims, the yellow-handled hammer used in many of their crimes and featured in the twisted videos, and computer storage devices. Igor had the hubris to clip out and keep newspaper articles relating to robberies and murders carried out by him and his friends. He also had a copy of Adolf Hitler's *Mein Kampf* on his bedside table.

Once under arrest, all three were quick to crumble and confess to their crimes, although later there were questions raised about the methods used by Ukrainian police to extract those confessions. Video released to the press showed Alexander Hanzha, the only one without influential parents, obviously severely beaten. There were no marks on either Igor or Viktor.

In Viktor's videotaped confession, the boyish-looking monster first said he acted alone, but soon admitted that he was in the company of Igor. When the detective asked him how many they had killed, Viktor responded: "I don't know. I don't remember how many. Maybe nineteen."

Then the detective asked the question everyone wanted to know: "Why?"

Viktor seemed unable to answer, at first saying that he didn't know why and eventually saying that he killed for money. But, he volunteered of his partner's motive: "Igor... Igor liked to kill."

Detectives soon determined that Igor was the ringleader of the trio and very likely a psychopath. When a detective asked Igor what he felt when he murdered innocent people, Igor answered dispassionately: "What do you feel when you cut a sausage?"

Igor told police he was ready to confess to the murders he had done "with my partner in crime, Viktor." In a video-taped interview he offered to show them the video of the murder of Sergei, which he had at home, having copied it from Viktor's phone. When asked why Viktor had recorded the killing, Igor responded simply: "To remember."

By the end of the day, Igor and Viktor had confessed to killing at least nineteen people in the previous four weeks. By the time formal charges were laid, the three men were charged with involvement in 29 separate incidents, including 21 murders and eight more attacks where victims survived. Igor was charged with 27 of the cases, including 21 counts of capital murder, eight armed robberies, and one count of animal cruelty. Viktor was charged with 25 instances, including 18 murders, five robberies and one count of animal cruelty. Alexander was charged with two counts of armed robbery from March 2007, after which he claimed to have withdrawn from the activities of his psychotic friends.

Once the arrest was made, the Ukrainian people were outraged as they heard the litany of crimes about which they had been kept in the dark. Despite the spate of brutal murders all carried out in the same manner, the city of Dnepropetrovsk had not warned its citizens, nor did they put a curfew into effect. Although some individual crimes made the local papers, there had been no major news stories of people being randomly attacked, murdered, and muti-lated by a serial killer. Had they been told, most people would take more precautions. If there had been news stories after young Vadim and other witnesses had come forward, everyone would have been wary of two young men stopped on the side of a lonely road or otherwise behaving suspiciously.

The people were now untrusting, and soon more rumors circulated that police had not caught all the perpetrators. In particular, there was the matter of Danil Kozlov, Viktor Saenko's close friend since kindergarten. He was known to hang out with Igor and Viktor, with neighbors recalling many times that the green Daewoo would pull up outside his house and honk for him to join the occupants. He had been arrested; some reports say for the murders, others for "hooliganism." He too was the son of a powerful and well-connected father with ties to officials. Kozlov had known about the trio's activities since they had come home from a vacation in the village of Kirilovka in early June 2007 and excitedly told him that they had killed two people. He had seen the video and pictures of their crimes. Kozlov told police everything he knew. He revealed how they boasted to him that they robbed and killed random people and urged him to join them, saying there was the prospect of making a lot of money. The boys showed him the expensive computer equipment that the three of them had, which they claimed were rewards of their crimes.

The information Danil provided to police, along with the testimony of two surviving victims, was the main thread upon which the investigation was based. He spilled all he knew about Igor and Viktor, and was never charged with anything, although at the very least he had concealed the heinous crimes. People thought that it was quite likely that Danil was involved in at least one murder, but the combination of his willingness to talk and his rich and well-connected family meant that he was never charged and soon disappeared. Unsubstantiated reports were that he killed himself soon after providing his evidence. Others believe he was whisked away so as not to have the family name dragged into any further scandal.

SINS OF THE FATHERS

Whilst the Ukrainian people and families of the victims fumed, the parents of the three accused rallied around them. Alexander's single mother had no influence or contacts, but Igor and Viktor's parents threw all of their resources and connections into setting their sons free. They maintained firmly that their sons were innocent of all crimes and were the fall guys for the true criminals, whose power and wealth provided them with immunity.

Their interference was met with considerable skepticism. Newspapers reported that Viktor Saenko's parents refused to open the door for at least forty minutes on the day of his arrest, and one report said that neighbors heard the sewer pipe rumbling in their apartment. The next day, according to that report, a plumber extracted watches, cartridges, and three mobile phones, which belonged to three of the murder victims. It is possible that this journalist had confused other reports that claimed it was Alexander Hanzha's plumbing that was dismantled to discover the stolen property. It is notable that Hanzha was not charged with any murders, but perhaps Igor and Viktor either sold or gave Alexander the valuables they stole from their victims.

Alexander's mother told reporters that there had been a mistake in arresting her son. Ironically, she said, "He is a kind boy. He couldn't hurt a cat, let alone a person."

Viktor's father told them, "I don't know why my son is admitting to these charges. He's an ordinary boy. I think that he must have been intimidated by someone. These charges have been fabricated."

Igor, in particular, was confident that his parents would fix this situation, just as they had bailed him out of every bit of trouble he had ever been in throughout his lifetime. When his lawyer asked if he had any messages for his parents, he responded that he missed his mother and that he would be back home soon. Journalists were worried that he was right, knowing that his father had been the personal pilot to Leonid Kuchma, and wondered if he would call upon the former Ukrainian president to help his son.

It is feasible that under normal circumstances in 2007 Ukraine, Igor's confidence would not be misplaced. Money would be paid, evidence would be lost, eyewitnesses would go silent, and the sons of the powerful would go free. However, there was something different in this case that meant releasing Igor and Viktor would be politically impossible. Among the items recovered by police in their raids on the boys' homes were hundreds of photographs and videos of the two young assassins carrying out their crimes and posing arrogantly with their victims. There was everything from an extended video of the torture of a kitten to selfies taken at the funerals, flipping off the coffin; from photographs of the two with dogs and cats strung up in trees, skinned alive, to photos with the freshly mutilated corpses of their human victims. Across one photograph, someone had scrawled: "The weak must die - the strongest will win." There were at least five videos documenting murders. A thirty-minute film showed the young psychopaths preparing, waiting for, and then murdering and mutilating the gentle Sergei Yatzenko.

Undeterred, Viktor Saenko's father insisted that the photographs and footage were faked. He told reporters that when police raided his house, they found perfectly innocent pictures and videos of Viktor with his friend Igor in the woods and that someone who wanted to frame them made up photos and videos using special effects and Photoshop.

Somehow, eight minutes of footage showing the final brutal moments of Sergei's life made its way from the evidence room to the internet. For those who could stomach watching it, there was no doubt that the giggling psychopath was Igor Suprunyuk, and his friend Viktor Saenko was behind the camera. Experts agreed that faking all footage found would require a Hollywood-level special effects team and a year of editing. Nevertheless, the boys' parents clung to the spurious claim.

As Ukraine waited for the trial, law enforcement and media alike tried to establish a motive for the killings. Robbery did not provide an adequate explanation because many of their victims obviously had nothing worth stealing. Vagrants and young boys going fishing were not people who would typically be expected to be carrying valuables.

With the release of the video of Sergei, another theory began to circulate. Local media reported that the killers had a plan to get rich by selling the murder videos they recorded to an underground snuff ring. The girlfriend of one of the boys reported that they planned to make forty separate videos of murders. This was corroborated by a former classmate who claimed he often heard Igor was in contact with an unknown "rich foreign website operator" who ordered forty snuff videos and would pay lots of money once they were made.

The theory that the maniacs were making films at the behest of a deranged millionaire who paid them to on-sell to shadowy figures was a popular one, and several journalists tried to verify the existence of a snuff network. One news crew claimed to find a site with the help of a Russian hacker that contained hundreds of murder videos, many of them made in Ukraine. But their efforts led nowhere, and the story was likely a fantasy woven around the video of Sergei's murder, which had reached viral proportions on the shock sites under the name *3 Guys, 1 Hammer*. It should be noted that someone with access to court records leaked the footage, not the maniacs themselves.

Shortly after their arrest, the three young men had psychiatric evaluations that returned findings that all three were sane and fit to stand trial. Nevertheless, Igor's lawyer tried to mount an insanity defense and insisted that his client should be treated, not punished. Igor had a paternal grandmother with schizophrenia, and his lawyer argued that Igor had inherited the condition. The lawyer disputed the court's psychiatric evaluations, saying that the notoriety of the crimes meant the defendants could not get fair treatment and the results were rushed and biased. Igor pleaded not guilty by reason of insanity.

TRIAL

The trial of Igor Suprunyuk, Viktor Saenko, and Alexander Hanzha began in June 2008 but was delayed after the first day when Igor's lawyer quit, unhappy that the court had not accepted his client's insanity defense. When he failed to convince the court of Igor's hereditary schizophrenia, he pulled out of the case citing his own health reasons.

Viktor's parents fired his lawyer, and his own father took on the defense. Viktor's lawyer was happy to be dismissed, saying that his client's story had changed and that he felt he could no longer provide him an adequate defense. Viktor, under the guidance of his father, recanted the confession he had made in the police station, saying it had been forced out of him through the use of violence and coercion. The case was adjourned until the new defense teams could get acquainted with the case file. There were whispers that Papa Saenko explored other methods of freeing his son, including pressuring at least one of the surviving victims not to testify.

The trial recommenced in early July. The three accused had to be transported to and from the courtroom wearing body armor as there was a very real fear they would be attacked by either families of the victims or the general public who despised them. They were put into a cage like feral animals, from where they could observe the proceedings. Igor and Viktor were allowed access to their parents who formed part of their defense teams, but Alexander's mother was denied any contact with her son.

Ten lawyers represented twenty-nine family members of victims who would be eligible for compensation from the crimes. The prosecution's evidence included eyewitness testimony, the many items belonging to the victims that had been recovered from the homes of the defendants, and DNA evidence that confirmed with over 99% accuracy the involvement of the accused in the murders. But the most compelling evidence was the photographs and videos produced by the suspects themselves. The court had a psychologist on standby when these exhibits were presented, and the counselor was put to good use. The relentless procession of slaughtered, torn animals and crushed heads of the victims of the hammer saw several people run from the courtyard sobbing, distraught in the face of such cruelty. The videos of the torture of a white kitten and the murder of Sergei Yatzenko and others were played in full, much to the distress of the families of the victims. Elderly Lidia Mikrenischeva watched her own teeth being viciously kicked in over and over by the giggling cowards as she lay on the ground, her dogs barking in the background.

Only the killers gazed calmly from behind the bars on the TV screen, occasionally exchanging glances and smirking at each other. When it came time for them to be questioned about the videos, however, they denied they were involved and said they did not recognize anyone in the footage, despite the many shots in which they mugged in close-up to the camera. The judge did not appreciate the court being played for a fool and responded indignantly, "You are not blind!"

The defense team for Igor and Viktor tried every tactic from having the photos and videos thrown out of evidence, due to them being obtained by an improper search, to a massive conspiracy cover-up to protect the 'real culprits' who they said were rich and famous. They argued that the confessions had been obtained through torture, although only Alexander had shown any signs of being beaten up.

When it came their turn to testify, the Dnepropetrovsk Maniacs turned on each other. According to Papa Saenko, Viktor was himself a victim, terrified of the psychotic Igor, who had forced him into participating in the slaughter. He claimed a sort of Stockholm syndrome and an ever-growing psychological dependence on Igor, arising from the fear the enigmatic younger boy had instilled in him since before they were teenagers. Viktor claimed Igor had made both direct and implied threats of violence and that he had convinced him that he could ensure all of the blame fell upon Viktor should they ever be caught.

Alexander's defense was that he was only involved in a single robbery prior to the murderous spree, to which he pleaded guilty. He claimed that he had no idea what Igor and Viktor were capable of and, if he had known, he would not have gone near them, even at gunpoint.

Igor, meanwhile, was generally silent throughout the trial, although he seemed to enjoy the replaying of his exploits on video. His mother formed part of the defense team, and families of the victims would later say they felt intimidated by her cold, unwavering stare and complete lack of sympathy when they spoke.

The one thing the prosecution could not come up with was a motive. The lack of motivation, coupled with the extreme cruelty, made this case unique. They accepted that profit from robbery was not their purpose, due to the number of victims who had no money or valuables. The rumors of the creation of videos for sale to the snuff market were not addressed at all, which led many people to believe there was a cover-up for wealthy, powerful individuals who commissioned the footage. Eventually, the prosecution settled on the unthinkable: Igor and Viktor tortured and killed people simply for the thrill and filmed their exploits to have mementos to look back on and enjoy in their old age.

On February 11, 2009, the court found Igor Suprunyuk and Viktor Saenko guilty of all charges of premeditated murder, robbery, and animal cruelty. Igor was found guilty of 21 murders, and Viktor 18. They both received life sentences, which they immediately appealed but which were upheld later that year by the Supreme Court. Alexander was found guilty of robbery and sentenced to nine years in prison. He did not appeal.

SEARCHING FOR ANSWERS

E ven after the trial had concluded, the people of Dnepropetrovsk were unsatisfied. They felt there had been irregularities, incompetence, and cover-ups in the investigation. They remained angry that the authorities had not disclosed that serial killers were on the loose in their city. But most of all, people wanted to know: how had these monsters come to be? They had wealth, privilege, and parents who loved them. They wanted for nothing, but something clearly went very wrong as early as elementary school.

Many blamed an increasingly permissive society, along with working parents being too busy to take note of what their children were getting up to. Modern life dictated that children were not receiving the love and attention necessary for a healthy upbringing, and parents were oblivious when their kids fell into bad crowds. Children were left unsupervised on computers and allowed to view material that desensitized them to violence. They played video games where characters could be mortally wounded, and in the next moment, up and about as if nothing had happened.

Nobody could believe that the parents had been blissfully unaware of what Igor and Viktor were getting up to. They were accused of spoiling their boys rotten and turning a blind eye to their misdeeds and the bloodstained clothes, the electronics and jewelry that suddenly appeared, letting them run wild while they attended their important jobs. When Yelena Shram's mother accosted Igor's mother, the latter reportedly looked her right in the eye and said, "Maybe your daughter was just destined to die."

The grieving mother told reporters later: "If it was up to me, I would dismember them into pieces, but the justice system won't let me do it."

The mother of returned serviceman Yegor Nechvolod reported a similarly cold response from Igor's mother, about whom she said: "No job can be an excuse for mental deafness to your child. How could you not feel the changes in the moods of the children, not see the deformation of their interests, not pay attention to the completely bloodstained clothes? How did you not look under the bed where the murder tools were stored and ignore other people's things suddenly appearing in your house, or the appearance of guns and bullets?"

Disturbingly, the Dnepropetrovsk Maniacs gained celebrity status among many young people. Teenagers were heard bragging that they attended the same school as the pair. In 2011, copycat killers cited Igor and Viktor as their inspiration when they killed six people in Russia, using hammers as their weapon of choice.

According to Ukrainian news reports in April 2019, Alexander Hanzha was released from prison, and by then was 31 years old, married with two children. The reports also put Igor in the Dnepropetrovsk detention center, and Viktor in the Krivoy Rog prison, serving out what will hopefully be life sentences.

The Dnepropetrovsk Maniacs destroyed many more lives than those of the 21 known murder victims. Vadim Lyakhov was traumatized for life having been subjected to horrors no 14-year-old could come away from unscathed. Andrei's grandmother continued to wear black and visit his grave, willing the young boy back to life, and sometimes Vadim went with her to the cemetery. He brought his friend field flowers and told him that the Maniacs had been caught.

Natalia Ilchenko lived so close to the site of her daughter's murder that she had to pass by almost every day. She would say a prayer for her daughter but felt nothing but hatred for her murderers. She told reporters: "You can't even call them animals because animals kill in self-defense, by instinct, or when they sense danger. They did it just for pleasure. They killed people for fun."

There are orphans who have to live with grandparents, parents who never recovered from the loss of their child, survivors who could never sleep through the night again. But worst of all, Sergei Yatzenko's family has to live knowing that a video of his torture and murder is still being shared around the worldwide web as a form of entertainment. It has entered internet folklore as being the ultimate test of a person's appetite for violence and gore. It has become a meme.

In 2012, a new video was uploaded to the gore sites with the claim that it was the sickest video ever to hit the internet. The video was called *1 Lunatic 1 Icepick* as an homage to the now-infamous *3 Guys 1 Hammer* and depicted the dismemberment of a young man, student Lin Jun. The murderer himself, a former male porn star in his twenties named Luka

Magnotta, uploaded the video. Like the Maniacs, Luka started on kittens, posting clips of himself torturing the tiny animals in a variety of ways and enjoying the notoriety the uploads earned him, even if he was almost universally reviled for his exploits. Luka craved attention, and the murder and dismemberment were his attempt to dislodge *3 Guys 1 Hammer* from its position as the goriest internet video of all time. He also went a step further in his quest for fame by sending pieces of Lin Jun's body to local politicians and a primary school.

The sick competition attracted thousands of downloads and heated debate as to which one was the most depraved. The two clips became the most popular choices for "reaction videos" – a craze where people film others (or sometimes themselves) watching a notorious video just to capture their reaction and upload the results.

In *1 Lunatic 1 Icepick*, Magnotta decapitates and dismembers Lin Jun, sodomizes his headless torso, and encourages a puppy to feast on his remains. Despite his efforts, *3 Guys 1 Hammer* has come out ahead as the most unwatchable, as Sergei is clearly alive throughout his ordeal and for many people, the sound is more distressing than the video. *1 Lunatic 1 Icepick* begins after the murder has already been carried out; the killing itself not captured.

In a depressing quirk of human nature, more people claim to be sickened by Luka's kitten torture videos than they are of the defilement of Lin Jun's corpse. Similarly, those who can watch the murder of Sergei can't stomach the prolonged torture of a kitten nailed to a crucifix.

Many people, like Caitlin Moran did at the beginning of this section, click on such videos unaware of their contents and forevermore wish they hadn't. For some people who deliberately seek out gore videos, *3 Guys 1 Hammer* is the one that crosses the line, makes them rethink their entertainment habits, and perhaps give up on the snuff-seeking.

But look at any of the hundreds of shock sites that host the video, and some comments make you despair for humanity. Some are obvious trolls, looking for a reaction, like the viewer who wrote: "I found it amusing. I love the sounds the victim makes as he draws his last few breaths. It made me ejaculate all over my keyboard the first time I saw it."

Others show a chilling lack of empathy that may be symptomatic of our times: "I do think this video is 'fucked up', but it doesn't bother me, it's just entertainment. Why else would anyone be here if they didn't find this type of video entertaining?"

Proud, brave Sergei Yatzekno, faithful husband, loving father, doting grandfather, beloved for his generosity and kindness has left an unthinkable legacy: he will forever be known as the faceless victim from *3 Guys, 1 Hammer*.

PART II

KILLER PETEY

PEDRO RODRIGUEZ FILHO

A YOUTUBE SENSATION

The YouTube video shows a pleasant-looking man who seems to be in his late 50s or early 60s. He's laughing and chatting with the unseen cameraman in Portuguese as he signs copies of his newly-released autobiography. His job today is to sign 500 copies for his most ardent fans. His YouTube channel has been exploding in popularity and he has over eight million views and 125,000 subscribers.

Since its humble beginnings 14 years ago, YouTube has become an unstoppable phenomenon. It's the second-most-popular website in the world, with visitors watching over a billion hours of video every day. The website's extraordinary reach has been responsible for creating celebrities out of nobodies, launching the careers of people who could never hope for access to traditional broadcast media, and cata-pulting people into superstardom overnight. Sometimes this is for conventional talents, such as singing, speaking, or acting. Some people prove themselves as adept tutors of anything from guitar to home renovations to makeup to knitting, building solid fan bases for their tutorials. Some of the most-watched YouTube channels are simply people playing video games. Then there are the fads: everything from people carrying out ridiculous, and often dangerous, challenges to the simplicity of children unwrapping their new toys, a trend known as "unboxing".

The popularity of such videos on YouTube has created some very unlikely superstars. Who would ever have imagined that there would be people becoming millionaires simply by livestreaming themselves playing video games or unwrapping toys? But while gamers, unboxers, and knitting tutors might seem to be improbable internet stars, they pale in comparison to the first celebrity serial killer.

Social media has its way of intensifying our society's infatuation with fame and notoriety. This "cult of celebrity" can extend to those who tread the darkest paths. This curiosity, sometimes labeled as "hybristophilia," signifies an attraction towards those who have enacted violent crimes. The barriers of society that would usually repel us from such individuals crumble in the face of digital distance and anonymity.

The past decade has witnessed a voracious appetite for true crime across various media platforms, YouTube being no exception. True crime podcasts, documentaries, and even amateur investigations are a significant driver of internet traffic, delving into the bewildering psychology and meticulously planned actions of murderers. This peculiar immersion can breed a bizarre fanbase, transforming criminals into dark celebrities, stars of their unnerving narrative.

Still, usually such content is *about* killers, not *by* killers.

Serial killers are psychopaths, the ultimate boogeymen. They are often shrouded in mystery and we hear of cruel tortures and victim ordeals that nightmares are made of, ritualistic murders, and possibly necrophilia and cannibalism thrown in for good measure. They are evil and kill without empathy and remorse. Anyone, no matter how innocent or blameless, could find themselves at the mercy of such a sadistic monster if they fit the murderer's criteria, and the chances of escape are slim. Serial killers are, without a doubt, Very Bad People.

How is it, then, that a serial killer with over 70 murders to his name, could be legally walking around free? How is it that during his years in prison he could keep on killing, all the while receiving letters of support, love, marriage proposals, and special requests for specific murders from people who never met him? How is it that since his release, that same serial killer has become a folk hero, has started his own YouTube channel that has an ever-growing fan base, as networks scramble to work with him to make films and documentaries about his life? How can there be, in this day and age, such a creature as the Superstar Serial Killer?

This is the tale of one such unlikely morbid celebrity. This is the story of Killer Petey.

DISCLAIMER

Killer Petey has been interviewed many times over the years. His official body count is 71, but he claims it is much higher, well over one hundred. He says there are many murders he was never charged with – mostly gang members in the favelas of Brazil in the late '60s and early '70s.

In interviews, specifics change often and he sometimes seems to confuse his stories from one account to another. He is prone to exaggeration, as many serial killers are, and boasts of incidents and murders that may or may not have happened. Stories of occurrences that have been independently verified sometimes change in the details.

Recently he released his autobiography, Pedrinho Matador. Right from the start, he seems to be mixing fact and fiction, claiming to be born at the stroke of midnight on October 30, when his date of birth is listed elsewhere as being in either June or July. It seems likely that Killer Petey is trying to create a legend whereby the boogeyman was born at the very beginning of Halloween. His number of siblings sometimes changes between interviews too, as does the tale of his first murder.

All I can do is relay the story as truthfully as possible, using stories told by Killer Petey himself in interviews and his book, along with reports from news sources about incidents at the time they happened. I hired a Portuguese translator and where I have quoted directly from his book, I have been as accurate I can, but some errors or misunderstandings may have slipped through.

I did contact Killer Petey on social media to clarify some things, but when he slipped into my DMs, I rethought the wisdom of that level of research.

A GRIM CHILDHOOD

In 1954, Pedro Rodrigues Filho came into the world with a misshapen skull. The deformity to the little boy came from a kick aimed deliberately and directly at the pregnant belly of Manuela Filho by Pedro Senior in one of the many violent altercations between the two. Pedrinho, as he came to be called, was lucky to be born at all, given the violence inflicted by his father upon his mother throughout their marriage, including when she was pregnant with Pedrinho and, no doubt, with many of the seven brothers and sisters who followed him.

Pedrinho grew up on a farm located in the Brazilian municipality of Santa Rita de Sapucai, south of the state of Minas Gerais. The family was poor, though perhaps not to the extreme level of poverty that could often be experienced in rural Brazil in the '50s and '60s. Food was neither scarce nor plentiful. The children didn't have to fight for scraps at every meal, but they had only enough to ensure they didn't go hungry. However, poverty surrounded them and was generally associated with criminality and high death tolls. Clean water was mostly diverted to be used elsewhere for the crops and a lack of sanitation led to diseases for which there was no money to treat. The poor were often viewed as disposable and life was cheap.

Many people, including Pedrinho's mother, were devoutly religious. Pedrinho would accompany her to church as often as he could, but he never understood what the pastor was saying and often fell asleep, earning him a beating. A common saying in the area was that God must exist because the Devil certainly did.

Pedro Senior worked hard for a meager salary and was an agreeable man until he started to drink, when he turned into the sort of monster who would violently beat his pregnant wife. Manuela, for her part, ruled the children with an iron fist and a bible; quick to punish and not afraid to administer beatings when Pedro or his brothers stepped out of line.

Pedrinho lived a grim life with his parents and younger siblings, but he was closer to his grandparents who provided him with much-needed affection. His grandfather, Joaquim, whom Pedrinho described as 'a simple gentleman', taught the little boy all the skills he would need to survive: how to swim, plant, harvest, hunt, and defend himself. He took the boy to work with him at the butcher shop, where he taught him how to handle a knife, de-bone an ox, and cut it into pieces. In his autobiography, Pedrinho wrote (translated from Portuguese): "He also taught me how to be a worthy, correct and just man. My grandfather loved me. Of all the grandchildren I was the dearest."

His grandmother, he would later claim, taught him that drinking ox blood would give him strength. He told Ilana Casoy, author of the book *Serial Killers: Made in Brazil*: "It's good for your health! My grandfather died 98 years old, still strong."

Family was everything for the poor in Brazil, because it was usually all they had. As the eldest, Pedrinho felt he had to provide for the younger ones. All the boys in the area worked before, after, or instead of school to help out their families, and before he was ten, he was killing feral monkeys for their pelts and meat, and fishing to help feed his family. By the time he reached double digits, he was working in a chicken slaughterhouse, putting to use some of the skills that his grandfather had taught him.

He had grown into a tough, wiry teenager, smaller than most of the boys his age. What he lacked in stature, he made up for in steely determination and a lack of fear. But by far the most defining characteristic of Pedrinho was his sense of fairness and deep resentment of injustice, especially when that injustice was directed at him or his loved ones.

A COUSIN, AN INJUSTICE AND A SUGAR CANE PRESS

By the time Pedrinho was thirteen years old, violence was simply a part of his life. He saw it at home, where he tried to divert his father's rages away from his mother; he saw it in the streets where drug dealers fought for territory; and he saw it at his work, where animals were slaughtered without any regard for humane practices.

An incident in 1967 unleashed a new urge in Pedrinho. He was working with an adult cousin, who he didn't know very well and who owned a horse. Pedrinho took the horse for a ride without asking, though he claimed he had no intention of stealing it. His cousin was angry when he found the boy on his horse and punched him in the face, hard enough to cause him to become dizzy. Shocked, Pedrinho looked his cousin in the eye and said, "I'm going to kill you."

His cousin, older and bigger, merely laughed and then hit him again, piling humiliation on top of the pain. The usual desire for revenge welled up inside Pedrinho, but this time it was more. He felt he had done nothing wrong and the reaction of his cousin, an adult, was excessive and unfair on him, a boy. He didn't just want to hit his cousin back; he genuinely wanted to kill him. The injustice festered in Pedrinho for weeks. He saw his cousin several times, but there was never an apology or acknowledgment of the pain he had caused. Others in the family heard of the incident and laughed at Pedrinho for being weak.

Sugarcane was the dominant agricultural crop in the area, and Pedrinho's grandfather sometimes worked the sugarcane mill, where the noisy, smelly method of processing occurred. There were few safety standards applied to the heavy machinery and equipment necessary for the job. Grandfather would occasionally get his grandsons to come along and help him. On this day, Pedrinho was working with his cousin and the two were responsible for feeding the cane through the sugar cane press, a machine consisting of two rollers that crushed the brown juice out of the long hard stalks. Watching the heavy steel rollers rotating and flattening even the toughest stalks, Pedrinho had an idea.

Not letting on to the rage quietly bubbling inside of him, Pedrinho waited for just the right moment to calmly but resolutely shove his cousin into the sugar cane press, and then lean against him pushing with all his might in an effort to make his entire body pass through the rollers. Pedrinho's understanding of physics was not very sophisticated, so he was surprised to find that when his cousin's arm went through up to his shoulder, his body jammed up against the machine, and there was no way to feed the rest of him through. He tried pushing his cousin's head into the rollers, but the head was the wrong size and shape, so the rollers just spun against his skull without grabbing hold. Worried that he would be spotted before the deed was finished, Pedrinho picked up some pruning shears and began to stab his cousin, hoping to cut him enough so that he would pass through the rollers and come out flattened on the other side.

There was no luck. Pedrinho's cousin merely remained trapped, his mangled arm on the other side of the rollers. Workers who heard the screams raised the alarm and shortly after, the boys' grandfather came to his rescue, turning the machine off.

Pedrinho was made to spend a couple of nights in jail, but his family needed him back out to work and provide for them. His grandfather came to the police station and told them the family did not want charges pressed, and as the boy was a minor, he was released back into their care. Pedrinho was made to clean the machine of the blood and flesh of his cousin as punishment, a job he said took him four weeks to do properly. He felt no remorse for crippling his cousin. He would often tell the tale, laughing with amusement, saying it gave him pleasure to do it as he had righted an injustice.

The incident had whetted the pleasure of revenge inside of Pedrinho and something more. He wanted to know what it would be like to kill somebody.

PEDRINHO'S FIRST KILL

A year later, when Pedrinho was fourteen, a calamity hit the family. Pedro Senior was laid off from his job as a night janitor at a local school, with no severance pay. He had been accused of stealing food and stationery from the kitchen during his patrols, which were from 6:00 PM to 6:00 AM every night.

Even when Pedro Senior was working, having enough food was not always guaranteed. The loss of the job meant the family definitely went hungry and would also certainly lead to an increase in drinking and the resulting violent outbursts by Pedro aimed at his wife. He told his family that it was not he, but one of his colleagues, the daytime guard, who had stolen the items. When the thefts were discovered, the daytime guard told the bosses that it was Pedro Rodrigues who was the thief.

Pedro Senior had sworn to his employers that he was innocent of the crime, but his pleas fell on deaf ears. He was fired and branded a thief, which meant he would never get another security guard position. Unemployed, he was unable to provide for his family, who had to get by on the money Manuela made by being a maid and laundress in the homes of well-off people. Pedrinho took to the jungle, hunting monkeys to sell for their pelts; the hides of capuchin and howler monkeys could be turned into fine leather which would then be turned into goods bought by the types of people his mother worked for. His grandfather had taught him to use a rifle, and he enjoyed both the hunt and the kill.

Even with Pedrinho's help, things got worse for the family and he would often come across his mother crying. The worst part to Pedrinho was the injustice of it all. Those with the means to feed his family refused to listen to his father's side of the story. His father had worked there for twelve years, and the headmistress and the deputy mayor, the man with the power to hire and fire the guards at the school, took the word of the other man without analyzing the evidence. The familiar feeling of revenge welled up inside of him, but this time he was going to do something about it.

Once again Pedrinho visited the shed where his grandfather kept his firearms. He took the rifle, plenty of ammunition, a machete and a tent, throwing it all into a green army backpack. He went into the mountains and built a camp there, where he could plan what he was going to do. In his autobiography he wrote, "I set up the tent and stayed there for about thirty days. My friends were the animals: monkeys, rabbits, snakes, and jaguars; they stayed there close to me, surrounded me, but they didn't hurt me. During my time in the woods I only killed what I had to eat, what was necessary to survive. I never exploited the woods and I never mistreated the animals. But I didn't go there to live, or to hide from my problems. When I got the guns, I had a plan and I already knew what I was going to do. I was going to get revenge."

It was a cold night as Pedrinho lay in wait for the deputy mayor outside his house, fingers clutched around his grandfather's loaded .36-caliber rifle. The jeep that rumbled up to the house was the sort of car only rich people drove. The deputy mayor turned in surprise at the sound of the gunshot that rang out as he got out of the car. Pedrinho lifted the gun and shot at him again, killing him instantly. Then he ran.

At fourteen years old, Pedrinho Rodrigues Filho had killed a man who had harmed his family. When Pedrinho killed chickens and monkeys, he felt nothing. No compassion, no empathy, just indifference. But this was different.

He felt righteous.

He felt pleasure.

Pedrinho was an avenger, and he would avenge the wrongs done to him and his loved ones.

PEDRINHO CARTUCHEIRA

lthough killing the deputy mayor gave Pedrinho a feeling of justice, he still seethed at the unfairness done to his father. One man could have put a stop to the dismissal of Pedro Senior: that was the day guard, the true thief of the school lunches. If he had confessed, Pedrinho's father would not have lost his livelihood, and the family would not be so poor. But there was the day guard, still working at the school, while Pedro's family starved.

The second time came easy to Pedrinho. He had done it once; he knew how to use the gun. A month after the first time he killed, Pedrinho went to the school where his father had once worked and his enemy was still employed. He waited in the storeroom where the guard always started his day. When the guard arrived, Pedrinho pointed the gun at him and made him sit in a chair in the middle of the room.

According to the book *Serial Killers: Made in Brazil*, Pedrinho had decided that from that time on, he would explain to his victims why they were dying. He would make them understand that they had committed a wrong and were being punished for it. In the case of the thieving day guard, he claims to have looked right in the man's eyes and said: "Did you see what you did? It destroyed my family. My brothers are starving because of you. Is it fair that you did this?"

Realizing who he was, the guard began to sob, apologize and beg for his life. But the damage had been done and Pedrinho was hell-bent on revenge. Forgiveness was not part of his plan. He shot the guard twice, then piled the furniture and boxes from the storeroom on top of his body and set it alight, before scampering away into the morning.

~

AFTER THE SECOND MURDER, the heat was on the Rodrigues family and Pedrinho fled to take refuge in metropolitan Sao Paulo at his godmother's house. There the teenager met the woman who would be his gateway to drug trafficking, known as Botinha, or "Bootie", in the local community. She was the widow of a well-known drug trafficker and a gangster in her own right. Bootie used her beauty and influence in the region to attract adolescents and children to the criminal organization. Pedrinho was young and small, but cut a dashing figure with his mop of frizzy hair and lean, muscular body.

She took the boy into her home in Mogi das Cruzes, in central São Paulo, took his virginity and put him to work in the business, trafficking and dealing drugs. He didn't have any experience, but his relationship with the crime boss allowed Pedrinho, still a minor, to take on high positions in the drug trafficking hierarchy. Older and more experienced drug dealers were not quick to accept the fourteen-year-old on their turf and were jealous of his connection with Bootie. The girlfriend of one of his rivals warned the boy that he

should watch his back and be prepared for an ambush when he least expected it. From that moment, he was on high alert.

The ambush came at a local lagoon. Pedrinho had been lured to the swimming hole to escape the heat and smoke some weed with the boys. Walking down the incline toward the water, he noted that the others were armed and acting strangely. Before they got to the lagoon, Pedrinho pulled his own gun and made the others drop theirs. He demanded to know why they had been planning to kill him, but they turned and fled. As they ran for their lives, Pedrinho shot at them, killing two and putting the other into the hospital.

Whether they had been a genuine threat or Pedrinho was suffering from paranoia, wiping out the competition allowed the boy to mark his territory and show that even though he was young and small, he was not someone to be messed with. He became known as Pedrinho Cartucheira, or "Cartridge Petey" because of his weapon of choice, a two-shot twelve-gauge sawn-off pipe shotgun.

Nevertheless, Pedrinho still managed to trust some people. He worked with friends "Gauchinho" and "Zé Capeta" and the three boys had each other's backs, sometimes quite literally as they took turns staying awake as the others slept. The trio carried out numerous crimes including one in Jacareí, an industrial town located between the cities of São Paulo and Rio de Janeiro. They were supposed to collaborate with a drug dealer who went by the name "China," but Pedrinho took an immediate dislike to him as a bully and a cheat, and decided to rip him off instead. Pedrinho and his cohorts stole China's drugs and guns and sold them to another dealer, somebody Pedrinho respected. It didn't seem like too big a deal at the time, but it was a decision that would come back to haunt Pedrinho.

$\backsim$

IT WASN'T JUST rival gang members Pedrinho had to worry about. He had become a prime target of Brazil's notorious death squads, comprising off-duty police officers and other members of the state security forces, which emerged in the late 1960s in Rio de Janeiro and São Paulo. Essentially vigilantes, they roamed the streets with the stated aim of ridding the slums of crime. This meant killing drug dealers, vagrants and street children, with the covert approval of the military government and invariably without consequences to themselves. Pedrinho became transient, sleeping in cars, cemeteries and churches, as he had to hide from both the police and his enemies.

This phase of Pedrinho's life came to an abrupt end when Brazilian police executed Bootie during a drug transaction. The police had been tipped off by Bootie's enemies, and Pedrinho was also wounded in the shootout. Disturbed by the death of one of the few people he cared about, and in bad shape physically, Pedrinho ran to take refuge with some extended family.

BLACK MAGIC

When he arrived on the doorstep of his family, Pedrinho had a request – he wanted them to perform a ritual that would protect his body from his enemies.

The relatives who took Pedrinho in were practitioners of Candomble Macumba, a religion sometimes considered to be witchcraft or black magic. Others referred to it as "psychotherapy for the poor." The highly ritualized belief system encompassed spirit offerings, ceremonial dancing, and animal sacrifices. Participants would often report becoming possessed by spirits, and afterward claim to feel cleansed, both spiritually and physically. The most sacred and symbolic substance in the rituals was blood, which was thought to represent life's pure essence.

Pedrinho believed that being inducted into the faith would mean the spirits would protect him from his enemies. His uncle and aunt grilled him to ensure he knew what he was getting into. A core belief of their religion was that good and evil were irrelevant. As an adherent, Pedrinho would be taught to fully embrace his life purpose and to steer his life to accomplish that purpose, but to always be aware that any harms inflicted on another person would come back to the person who caused the injury. That philosophy sat well with Pedrinho's own sense of justice.

When Pedrinho insisted he wanted to go through with the ritual, his uncle made him gather together a coconut, with all of its hair carefully removed, gunpowder and a wick to put in the coconut, an all-black cat, and seven stringed beans. The Voodoo-like ceremony took place outdoors, as required by the faith, in a deserted quarry at midnight. Pedrinho had been shaved clean of his hair and eyebrows. The complicated ritual involved Pedrinho killing a cat and drinking its blood and then being covered in the remainder of the blood and entrails, while in a trance. The carcass was then filled with seeds and buried by Pedrinho. During the ritual, a dozen members of the religion surrounded the teenager, drumming and dancing. Pedrinho felt himself becoming possessed as the ceremony went on into the small hours of the morning.

He concluded the initiation exhausted but with the firm belief that he had become invincible. Knives would not pierce him and bullets would bounce off him. He did not need to fear his enemies or the death squads.

Exactly a week later he returned to the site, dug up the cat carcass and removed the seeds, which had hardened into beads. His uncle threaded them onto a string which he placed around Pedrinho's neck, warning him never to remove his new necklace. In his autobiography Pedrinho wrote: "From then on, the cops opened fire, but the bullets didn't hit me. The enemies attacked, and I defended myself with ease. Nothing would stop me. Before, I was afraid, but after [the ceremony] it was as if nothing could affect me."

From that moment on, Pedrinho wrote, he became a

defender of the weak and vulnerable. He hijacked food trucks, which he took into the slums to feed the hungry. He burned the shops of those who cheated the poor. He defended the honor of women, killing the men who cheated or harmed them, and the penalty for cruelty to animals was the same inflicted on the perpetrator.

Pedrinho was sixteen years old, and he was invincible.

THE RED WEDDING

Never wanting to stay in one place too long, especially if that meant putting his relatives at risk, Pedrinho moved to Campo Grande, a city in the west of the state of Rio de Janeiro. There he met and fell in love with a girl by the name of Maria Aparecida Olympia. When Maria became pregnant with his baby, Pedrinho moved with her into a modest shack, continuing his newfound career of stealing from the rich and giving to the poor, and stealing from the bad drug dealers to sell to the righteous ones. Pedrinho believed himself to be a vigilante and justified his crimes as being legally wrong but morally correct.

The legend of "Cartridge Petey" ran through the slums of Brazil's largest cities, where he came to be both admired and feared. Those he assisted, or who wanted to curry favor, protected him and warned him when trouble was approaching. But his body count meant that Pedrinho would always have enemies and could never let his guard down.

The sins of his past came back to haunt him when Maria was seven months pregnant. Pedrinho's world fell apart when he came home to find that someone had come to his house and slaughtered Maria and their unborn child, as well as the man Pedrinho had appointed to protect her. The murderers used Maria's blood to scrawl: "We will get you" on the wall.

Pedrinho had always felt that he was a righteous avenger, robbing from and killing only those who deserved it. But after the murder of the woman he loved and his unborn child, the need for vengeance burned in him like he never had before. He swore he would track down the murderer and have his revenge.

For more than a year, Pedrinho's life was spent making inquiries and torturing any people who were not forthcoming but who he thought might have an idea of who killed his wife and unborn child. He had murdered so many people and had so many enemies, he didn't know where to start looking. His inquiries seemed to be going nowhere until one day he stopped at a bar and was told there was a young woman looking for him. "She came from the Valley," he was told, and she drove a jeep. The Paraiba Valley was a region in the eastern part of the state of São Paulo and the western part of the state of Rio de Janeiro.

The young woman was the former wife of a drug dealer who went by the name China, a man from Pedrinho's past. She showed him scars, bruises, and burn marks that she said she suffered at the hands of China. The woman told Pedrinho: "It was China who ordered your wife's death."

As she told her story, Pedrinho was convinced she was telling the truth. China had never forgotten nor forgiven Pedrinho for stealing his guns and drugs stash, shooting one of his men, and injuring China and his brother, who had run away cowering. Pedrinho kicked himself for not having realized who the culprit was earlier.

China's vengeful ex-wife told Pedrinho that China's brother was getting married the following Saturday in Jacarei, the same place where Pedrinho had robbed the drug dealer two years earlier.

Pedrinho recruited the same two men who had visited Jacarei with him back then, Gauchinha and Zé Capeta, and told them they would be attending a wedding. Pedrinho's orders were simple: every man at the wedding was to get a bullet, but no women or children were to be harmed. "If you shoot them, you are going to have to deal with me," he told them.

Half a century before anyone had ever heard of *Game of Thrones*, Jacarei in Brazil had its very own Red Wedding. Pedrinho, Gauchinha, and Zé Capeta crept up on the revelers, who ate, danced, and drank, unaware of the presence of the teenager hell-bent on revenge outside the venue. As glasses clinked and music blared, the trio slipped in unnoticed, pretending to be invited guests. The unsuspecting wedding party was in full swing when Pedrinho knocked on the door to the reception hall. When an older man answered, Pedrinho told him: "I am an honored guest of China. I believe, the most awaited guest of the night."

Spotting China behind the man, the three burst in and overpowered China's father, and yelled at the women and children to go upstairs. Pedrinho was brandishing his trademark 12-gauge shotgun—or scattergun as he preferred to call it—when China came at him, pointing a .44. Pedrinho shot him straight in the chest, killing him instantly.

The death of China was not enough for Pedrinho, however. The men in his family were all gang members, complicit in his business, and as far as Pedrinho was concerned, they were every bit as guilty of Maria's murder as the drug dealer. He started shooting indiscriminately, using the cache of guns he had brought with him, and those of the men already killed. They shot until they had almost run out of ammunition, keeping only what they might need to make their getaway. Pedrinho and his friends calmly strode through the carnage, ignoring the screaming and begging of the wounded and stepping over the bodies of the dead. They left by the front door and went to a bar to have a drink.

Pedrinho ended up killing seven men and wounding sixteen that night. No children were harmed, and the only woman to sustain an injury was China's mother, to her arm, something Pedrinho said later was her own fault as she threw her arms around her son to try and protect him.

KILLER PETEY

After the wedding massacre, the legend spread throughout São Paulo and beyond. It earned the pint-sized teenager the nickname "Pedrinho Matador," literally "Little Pete the Killer," or "Killer Petey." He was the feared psychopath who killed without mercy or hesitation, the wronged man who sought the ultimate revenge for the murder of his lover and unborn child, but he was also the protector of women and children, ensuring they would not pay for the sins of their husbands and fathers.

According to his autobiography, Pedrinho hooked up with a pair of twins shortly after the wedding massacre, and they became a polyamorous threesome. He began to live the lifestyle of a cashed-up gangster. He loved his notoriety as Pedrinho Matador and his reputation as a fearless killer. He wrote: "I had money, morals, respect, and power." He enjoyed the fear that his presence caused on the street or the moment he entered a building, especially among those he considered scum—rapists, standover men who extorted local businesses, and those who preyed on the weak. He worked to make sure those sorts of criminals were more afraid of him than they were of the Death Squads.

On the inside of his right forearm, he tattooed the words: "I kill for pleasure." The phrase was added to the amateurish pictures of snakes, a heart with a dagger through it, skulls, knives, crosses, something resembling a potted plant on his chest, and random words the teen sought to have inked all over his body by friends, or which he did himself.

On his other arm, he tattooed Maria's name and the inscription "I can kill for love."

Pedrinho would later tell journalist Roberto Cabrini on *Conexão Repórter* that during this period he killed every day. If a day went by without him having killed someone, he said, he got agitated. He told the reporter: "I would summon the devil. It was a ritual. It was like, 'It's yours. This body is yours. This blood is yours.'"

Then he would kill his victim and drink his blood, believing as his Grandma taught him, that the blood of his enemies made him stronger.

But not even the corrupt police in the poor areas of Brazil could ignore that many bodies in a wedding party, and a manhunt began to track down those responsible. Brazil is a very large country with many places to hide, but Pedrinho had many enemies and those who would betray him. Both Gauchinho and Zé Capeta were killed during this time, the former by the police during a robbery and the latter by a death squad that was looking for Pedrinho. Pedrinho took cover where he could, but his paranoia grew, he could trust nobody, and he felt they were closing in on him.

Killer Petey was finally arrested on May 24, 1973. He was having a drink at the bar where the father of the twins worked when they swooped. The twins' father had ratted

him out. Pedrinho was taken down in a dramatic gunfight, badly wounded, passing out to the sounds of men screaming for his death.

When he awoke, he was chained to a hospital bed, surrounded by nurses, police, and news cameras, there to capture the moment Pedrinho Matador was charged with murder. At age 18, it seemed Killer Petey's murderous ways had finally come to an end.

PRISON

Pedrinho spent twenty-five days recovering in the hospital, chained to the bed and under 24-hour guard. He was all over the news, with the press fascinated by Killer Petey and his twisted sense of righteousness. When he was well enough to be moved into prison, he was provided with the option of going into protective custody or going into general population, where the friends, brothers, and sons of many of the men he had killed waited for his arrival. Pedrinho chose to go into the general population.

He enjoyed his newfound celebrity and was disappointed when he learned that he would only be charged with eighteen homicides, telling the court and reporters: "Only that? It cannot be that little." Pedrinho swore he had killed over a hundred men. In the end, he was convicted for just fourteen that could be properly pinned on him at the time. For those, he received a sentence of 126 years in prison.

When transferring Pedrinho to the jailhouse, the police put him in the back of the police wagon with another criminal, a serial rapist. By the time they got to their destination,

there was only one man alive in the back of the truck. Killer
Petey *really* hated rapists.

~

BRAZILIAN PRISONS HAVE a reputation for being some of the
toughest and most violent in the world, and during the early
1970s, it was even worse. The inhumane conditions were
overcrowded, unsanitary, uncomfortable, and unsafe.
Prisons were breeding grounds for infectious diseases like
tuberculosis and dengue fever. Prison guards at the very best
were considered insensitive, crude, inaccessible, and indif-
ferent. At worst, they were either sadistic monsters or thoroughly corrupt, ready to take a bribe and willing to break
any rules for anyone with enough money.

Araquara prison in Sao Paulo was one of the toughest.
Brutal bashings were a daily occurrence, and deaths were
almost as common. Prison gang warfare pitted criminals
from different cities against each other, and the resulting
battles would often end in prisoners being decapitated or
disemboweled in a display of power. There could be dozens
of prisoners in a single small cell where there was not even
enough room to lay down, wallowing in deplorable, unsanitary conditions. The problems that came with overcrowding
were exacerbated by boredom and idleness.

The underpaid and outnumbered staff largely left the
prisoners to their own devices, and they could do whatever
they wanted within the confines of the walls of the prison.
The guards would hand over the keys to internal locks to
whichever inmates were running the show, their job
confined to securing the outside of the prison. Prisoners
organized themselves into gangs, the largest of which
wielded enormous power, and they waged brutal turf wars.

For most inmates, the only way to stay safe was to join a gang that would provide protection, a certain amount of comfort, and even money for an attorney. It was child's play to smuggle in weapons and drugs, and even women on occasion.

Pedrinho entered prison young, even by Brazilian standards, where half of all male prisoners are aged between twenty and twenty-nine. The average life expectancy of a prisoner in Brazil was low, and it was almost unheard of for an inmate to remain alive in jail for fifteen years before being killed by either disease or an enemy.

Even though he must have heard stories of prison all his life, Pedrinho was completely unprepared for what awaited him. In his autobiography, he wrote: "By the time I went through processing, I began to understand what I would go through. The cell was small, there was no mattress, there was nothing, just the frozen concrete floor. There was no shower, it was just a water nozzle; there was no toilet, there was only a hole in the floor." What's worse, as the newest arrival, Pedrinho's sleeping spot was on the floor closest to the toilet hole.

He arrived with a huge target on his back. Not only were there members of gangs of the men Pedrinho had killed outside who were hell-bent on exacting revenge on behalf of their brotherhood, but he was also a high-profile celebrity thanks to the media interest both before and after his arrest. Jealousy and the desire for notoriety put Pedrinho in the sights of prisoners from all sides.

His reputation as a killer had already run through prison before he arrived. Pedrinho knew he had to watch his back and keep his wits about him. With the help of a cellmate, he improvised a knife fashioned from spoons sharpened to a deadly blade and made sure to have it with him at all times.

It wasn't long before the inevitable happened. The prison yard was hushed that day when Pedrinho entered. Five men were involved in the ambush on the killer teenager, and when they surrounded him, the crowd turned to look. The inmates were well-attuned to keeping to themselves and not poking their noses into others' business, but it was difficult to look away from what would surely be a bloody massacre.

It is not entirely clear what happened next. Eyewitness accounts are apocryphal, and Pedrinho's own recollections can be muddled or embellished. What we do know is that three of the men in the ambush were killed, and the other two were badly wounded, enough that they did not want to continue the fight and fled. The legend of Killer Petey increased tenfold within the Araquara prison.

It quickly became well-known that Pedrinho could and would kill without hesitation for any reason, and he wasn't afraid of anybody. Sometimes Pedrinho was able to get his hands on a weapon, whether that be a makeshift one such as a shiv fashioned out of any bits and pieces he found lying around the prison, to an illegally-obtained knife or firearm, which was not uncommon in the corrupt Brazilian prison system. Other times, it was his bare fists that were the weapon, with breaking necks a specialty. He taught himself martial arts, punching his cell walls until they were covered in his blood, training himself to withstand any sort of pain.

But Pedrinho was not the sort of person who was simply out of control, unable to curb his rage. Sometimes he had targeted somebody to kill, but for whatever reason, it was not the right time. Pedrinho would befriend them, share his food or meager belongings with them, even hug them. He would gain their trust over weeks or months before striking when they least expected it. Pedrinho's major advantage was

he was completely merciless. There was never any hesitation when he decided to kill someone, nor were there ever any regrets.

When he wasn't working out, he enjoyed the gambling that went on in the prison, where the stakes were high. He looked forward to the visits of his mother and grandmother, who came every week to check on him. Pedrinho may have had a thousand enemies, but at least he had two women he could be sure loved him no matter what.

THE CRUELLEST KILL

The night his world turned upside down again, Pedrinho had gone to bed early. His cellmates had been drinking, snorting cocaine, and gambling, but Pedrinho was feeling relaxed and sleepy, having had a joint straight after a visit from his mother earlier in the day. He had gotten up at one time to go to the bathroom, and he noted that some of his cellmates were acting strange. They turned down the radio to a whisper as he passed.

The radio was the prisoners' lifeline to the outside world. It played nonstop, so the inmates could keep up with a world that had forgotten them. Pedrinho noted the odd behavior and upon returning to bed, made sure his shiv was easily accessible.

The next day, things still seemed a little off. Pedrinho caught prisoners sneaking glances at him, and people stopped talking when he came near them, awkwardly changing the conversation. He went to an area of the yard that was used as a gym, where he filled plastic bottles with water and tied them at either end of a broomstick to use as weights and started his two-hour workout.

He was alone in the eerie silence when a guard came to tell him he was wanted in the Prison Director's office. He was handcuffed and taken to see the Director, flanked by two guards, sensing the eyes of everyone he passed boring into him. Even though Pedrinho had never attacked any of the prison staff, no doubt this time they wanted safety in numbers, as they were bearing very bad news for him indeed.

Manuela Filho had been killed; stabbed to death in her bed as she slept. It had been a frenzied attack, leaving a bloodied, mutilated corpse. The news that Pedrinho Matador's mother had been murdered had made it to the radio during the night, but nobody in the cellblock had wanted to be the one to tell Pedrinho.

Pedrinho found the news hard to take in. He had just seen his mother the previous morning. He warned the jailer that if he was kidding, it was not funny, and the Director was no doubt happy he had his armed backup with him at that moment, even if Pedrinho was handcuffed.

There was another bombshell to come. Pedrinho's father, Pedro Rodrigues, had been charged with the brutal murder and had been taken into custody.

The Director said they wanted to provide him with the opportunity to see his mother in the morgue before she was buried if he wanted. Pedrinho did want to. They took him, under heavy guard and leaving him in no doubt that if he made the slightest wrong move, he would be shot. He viewed his mother's body in a coffin, completely torn to shreds. When Pedro Sr. finally went too far, he went way, way too far. Manuela Filho had been hacked apart with a machete, stabbed twenty-one times in some sort of psychotic rage.

As he stood over his mother's coffin, Killer Petey made a

vow. He promised his mother that he would kill his father and eat his heart to avenge her death. For anyone else, these would be empty words. But Killer Petey routinely drank the blood of his victims. It was one of his signature moves until the AIDS epidemic in the 1980s scared him out of it.

A week later, Pedrinho was told that his aunt, his father's sister, had come to the prison and left a cake for him. Pedrinho divided the cake among his cellmates and gave a little to the stray dogs that some of the prisoners kept as pets. The next thing he knew, one puppy was vomiting, and another had fallen over. One of the prisoners who had taken a bite had also started vomiting.

The cake tested positive for poison. Police interrogated Pedrinho, and soon after, he was transferred to another penitentiary, the first of many such transfers for Killer Petey.

THE SINS OF THE FATHER

Pedro Rodrigues Sr. was convicted of the stabbing murder of his wife. As luck would have it, he was put into the same prison as his son, but in a different section, locked away for his own safety.

Pedrinho Matador has told the story of what happened next countless times. The details sometimes change, but the main facts are undisputed. One day, he called a guard to his cell, claiming illness. Using a large knife he had managed to acquire, he threatened the guard and took away his gun and his keys. He used the gun to shepherd other guards into a cell, which he locked. He then made his way to the cell block where his father was being held. Upon opening the cell door, the other inmates, seeing who had come in, promptly scattered. Pedro Sr. did not attempt to run. He stood in the corner, near the wall. As Pedrinho approached him, he said, "You are right, my son."

Pedrinho didn't want to hear anything his father said to him. The older man offered no resistance when Pedrinho lunged at him and wrestled him to the ground, straddling him with the knife held high. Pedrinho began stabbing his father, counting as he went. One, two, three... the sound the knife made each time it was pulled out kept his rhythm of counting going, as he reached double figures. When the numbers got into the high teens, he concentrated the blows on his father's chest area, as he worked toward his goal.

At number twenty-two, Pedrinho stopped. His father had stabbed his mother twenty-one times. Pedrinho wanted to be sure Pedro was stabbed one more time than his mother. As the blade went in the final time, Pedrinho felt an overwhelming sense of relief: it was right and good that his violent murderous father was dead. Killer Petey was the righteous avenger once again.

Then it was time to make good on his final promise to his mother.

Pedrinho dug around his father's chest cavity until he found his still-beating heart, wrenching the organ away from the warm corpse. He laid his father's heart on the ground, sliced off a sizable piece of meat, and popped it into his mouth, chewing vigorously.

It was so tough and chewy, he couldn't bring himself to swallow it, so he spat it out onto his father's body. He had what he came for: the ultimate insult and the ultimate vengeance.

Pedrinho stayed just a few seconds more with his father's body before making his way back to the cell where he had locked up the guards. He released them, handing over not only the guard's gun but his knife as well and allowed himself to be handcuffed and taken away.

THE PUNISHER

Killing his father did nothing to curb's Pedrinho's murderous ways. He figured he was going to be in prison for a very long time, so there was no need to be in prison with people he felt did not deserve to live. Pedrinho was an advocate for the death penalty, and he had appointed himself judge, jury and executioner for carrying it out. His moral code saw him targeting rapists, pedophiles, and the men who murdered women and children. His reputation, both from his life on the streets and then in prison, continued to grow. Some people nicknamed him "The Punisher", after the Marvel Comics character who employed murder, kidnapping, extortion, coercion, threats of violence, and torture in his campaign against crime.

Pedrinho kept to himself a lot of the time, but occasionally he would befriend fellow inmates. One such man, Claudio, had come into the prison needing protection, and Pedrinho provided it to him. When Claudio was due to be released, he promised Pedrinho that he would help him escape. Pedrinho gave him the address of his grandmother's house, where he would be welcomed and assisted. There,

Claudio met and started dating Pedrinho's sister, Silvana. However, one night, Pedrinho's brother disrespected Claudio, hitting him and accusing him of having had a sexual relationship with Pedrinho in prison. In rage and retaliation, Claudio fired shots, killing Silvana and wounding her friend.

When Claudio arrived back in prison, Pedrinho reassured him that he bore no grudge and it was understandable that the brother's words and actions set him off. The two had been close friends and Claudio relaxed in relief that Pedrinho would continue to protect him.

A short time later, Pedrinho visited Claudio in his cell. Claudio was studying and lifted his pen as his friend entered. Pedrinho wordlessly pulled Claudio's head back by the hair and went to work on his throat with his knife, stabbing, cutting and sawing until he was able to lift Claudio's decapitated head high in the air. He felt nothing, but his sister had been avenged.

"He was my friend, but I just had to kill him, I'm justified," he said later in an interview.

When he wasn't killing people, Pedrinho lifted weights and practiced martial arts, but most importantly he finally learned to read and write. Once he learned to read, he became an enthusiastic visitor to the library. He devoured the books of trashy fiction author Sidney Sheldon, but his favorite book was *Roots*, the classic and depressing story of a teenager sold into slavery.

His new skill also meant he could read the letters he received from the public about men who were locked away with him. People on the outside were requesting the help of Killer Petey to avenge the wrongs his fellow prisoners had done. If the writer seemed genuine enough, sometimes Pedrinho would carry out their request, but he refused to kill for money. He enjoyed choosing a victim and luring them into a trap, and had no problem pretending friendship right up to the moment when he would strike. He would either club them to death, stab them or break their necks. He threw one man down an elevator shaft because he had extorted the relatives of prisoners. His twisted form of celebrity spread throughout Brazil and beyond. He relished his reputation as the most feared and dangerous man in the history of the Brazilian prison system.

The letters of requests for murders turned into requests for relationships. Pedrinho claimed to get up to fifty letters every week: fan mail and love letters. He even received several marriage proposals. He was bemused that people would write to him and found it odd that women were attracted to someone like him. Mostly he ignored them, but he did strike up a relationship with a woman who was also in prison. They wrote to each other regularly over the years, and when she was released she would come to visit him.

The prison sent in psychiatrists to evaluate Pedrinho and they diagnosed him as a psychopath, incapable of feeling remorse or sympathy, with the added complications of paranoia and anti-social personality disorder. Psychiatrists who evaluated Pedrinho in 1982 wrote that the greatest motivation of his life was "a violent affirmation of self." Like most serial killers, Pedrinho kept all the newspaper clippings about his life and crimes that he could lay his hands on.

When he went before a judge for the murders he carried out inside the prison, the judge asked him for reasons for the killings. Pedrinho said: "I did not like his face," for one and "He snored too much," for another.

The press always attended court hearings of Killer Petey and the story of the serial killer murdering a cellmate for the crime of snoring too much entered into folklore. Many years later, he would tell reporter Roberto Cabrini that he was just being droll with the court and this wasn't true. He said that the real story was that after a riot in the prison, Pedrinho was put into a private room in a hospital. Due to overcrowding, it was necessary to place another inmate with him, and Pedrinho assured the guards that there would be no problem. A couple of days later, Pedrinho received a visit from his girlfriend. As the couple became amorous, he noticed that the second prisoner was staring at them. It was his disrespect and rudeness that got him killed, not his snoring.

Pedrinho's innate propensity to violence and his psychiatric problems were not helped by the Brazilian prison system. The conditions of squalor and boredom only exacerbated his issues and fed his paranoia, which meant his killing became for increasingly pointless reasons. Every time he was transferred - to nine different institutions - Pedrinho committed more crimes.

The story of Pedrinho Matador's most extreme incident is sketchy. He told the tale of breaking his own record of murders in one day in an interview with Roberto Cabrini for *Conexão Repórter*, but there doesn't seem to be any public record of the event in any other news sources.

The reporter said: "Pedrinho, tell me about the transsexuals night."

Pedrihno Matador told Cabrini that a transgender prisoner had been in love with a friend of Pedrinho, who did not return the affections. The prisoner spread a rumor about Pedrinho's friend, which resulted in him being killed. Pedrinho swore vengeance and rampaged through the section where the transgender prisoners were housed, stabbing and killing indiscriminately, until sixteen inmates lay dead. He told the reporter he had gone crazy "killing faggots" and was deaf for three days from all of the blood-curdling screams of the unsuspecting prisoners.

By this time, Pedrinho's official body count was seventy-one, and that was just the ones that could be confirmed and pinned on him. His cumulative sentence was now 400 years. The authorities decided enough was enough. Pedrinho was sent into a psychiatric ward, with orders that he was not to have contact with any other prisoners.

MAXIMUM SECURITY

In 1985, Pedrinho was transferred to Taubaté Maximum Security Prison and Psychiatric Treatment Center, about eighty miles outside Sao Paulo. The center boasted a custom-built annex, known as the "Piranha," designed to house inmates deemed too dangerous for the somewhat loose general prison system. At Taubaté, prisoners lived in minuscule cells, where they spent the majority of their day. They were allowed outside for exercise and out of their cells for meals, but only under stringent supervision.

The prison's methods proved effective. Killer Petey stopped killing. Pedrinho distracted himself with reading, writing letters, playing solitaire, and repeatedly punching the cell wall until he was allowed a bag of sand to punch instead.

At night, those he had killed sometimes returned to Pedrinho. His dreams were infiltrated by an assortment of creatures - panthers and tigers, rats and monkeys, but mostly snakes - and they would converse with him.

Pedrinho always recognized which man had come to him in disguise, and he would kill them again.

The one who returned most often was his father. Pedrinho told reporter Roberto Cabrini, "Sometimes I kill him again when he appears in my dreams. He would appear as a snake, speaking... He would seem to be a snake and, in my dream, he attacked me, biting me, and I would grab him and tell him: 'I killed you, that's correct, and I will kill you again.' And I would crush the snake that was speaking. It was a snake but it was my father, speaking."

In the early 1990s, a new prisoner was transferred to Taubaté. Former plastic surgeon Hosmany Ramos had been sentenced to fifty-three years in prison for theft of airplanes, car smuggling, and the murder of his personal pilot and a stewardess.

According to Pedrinho, Ramos had snitched to the wardens about a plan by a younger inmate to escape. When Pedrinho confronted him about it in the lunch room, Ramos punched him in the mouth. The next moment, Ramos was on the ground with Pedrinho's foot on his neck. Ramos was saved from death when the guards intervened.

From then on, Pedrinho ate in his cell.

A private war between Pedrinho and Ramos began. Some time later, Pedrinho claims to have received a cake through the bars from a fellow inmate. When he bit into it, he started to bleed from his mouth and was only saved after swallowing an entire can of powdered milk to detoxify. Pedrinho was sure it was Ramos who had sent the cake, but he never had another chance to see the other man. Ramos was eventually released and went back to practicing surgery.

From 1992 to 2002, Pedrinho was completely isolated, in a form of solitary confinement, where he only had contact with the jailers. Other inmates were permitted in the yard together for their hour of exercise, but Pedrinho was only allowed the company of two guards, who were ready to shoot him if he made a single wrong move. For a decade, Pedrinho's only human interaction was with the guards, to whom he was always polite and respectful, and the journalists who dared visit to interview him. He told one interviewer that the staff of the prison had nothing to fear from him because, he said, "I only kill scoundrels."

The press's interest in Pedrinho Matador had not waned. In August 1996, journalist Eduardo Faustini visited him in prison for an interview, which was recorded for TV. In it, the journalist asked Pedrinho if he was released, would he kill again. Pedrinho replied calmly, "Yes, I would have to. To put it simply, I'm a murderer. I always have been."

In 1998, another infamous inmate arrived at the prison. "Motoboy" Francisco de Assis Pereira, better known as the Park Maniac, had been accused of raping, torturing, and murdering eleven women in the State Park in Sao Paulo. Nine other women had been raped but not killed during his reign of terror. The Park Maniac found his victims by posing as a talent scout for a modeling agency. He was sentenced to 268 years in prison.

When asked about Motoboy by a reporter for a TV channel that had come to interview him, Pedrinho said, "Today my biggest dream is to be alone with him. My dream is to break that neck. What he did is unforgivable. He killed a lot of defenseless girls. I despise rapist murderers."

Pedrinho's declaration that he would kill the Park Maniac made headlines all over South America and won him even more fans. The prison's Director had to issue a statement assuring the public that, no matter how popular the idea was, there was no way Pedrinho would be able to keep that promise. Pedrinho was kept completely isolated, spending twenty-three hours a day in his cell, and using the exercise yard alone. The director told the press, "Even if Pedro can get out of the cell, he won't know where to find Francisco. Additionally, the two are always accompanied by prison guards."

On December 17, 2000, during visiting hours, a Taubaté Prison inmate opened fire on prisoners from a rival gang with a smuggled-in gun. Amid the ensuing chaos, the prisoners took control of the facility and took twenty-three hostages, including four children.

The inmates had seized control.

During the standoff, prisoners negotiated for the transfer of ten inmates to another facility in return for releasing the hostages. Through tense negotiations, hostages were released in small groups. At the same time, news started to trickle in that prisoners were being murdered, mostly as a result of rival gangs capitalizing on the situation to exact revenge on their enemies. Among those reported dead was the Park Maniac, a story swiftly seized upon by news networks. Everyone knew of Pedrinho Matador's threat, and it looked like he had made good on his promise and killed one of Brazil's most notorious serial killers in Brazil's highest security prison.

The rebellion ended just one day later, with all of the hostages released unharmed. They reported to the authorities that they had been treated well by their captors throughout the ordeal. Some were thrilled to reveal that Pedrinho Matador himself had been responsible for bringing food to them and keeping them comfortable.

The next day, the authorities reversed their initial report that the Park Maniac had been killed during the uprising. The Sao Paulo State Prison Administration Department clarified that Francisco Assis Pereira was alive. Prison authorities said they initially believed Pereira was dead because he had received frequent threats from other prisoners and was missing from his cell when the uprising began.

Pedrinho later told reporters that he wanted to kill the Park Maniac during the rebellion, but he had been occupied with looking after the hostages. His failure to fulfill his promise was met with disappointment from much of the public.

HOW DO YOU SOLVE A PROBLEM
LIKE KILLER PETEY?

In the early 2000s, the Brazilian authorities convened to discuss a rare, but very big, problem. Article 5 of the Brazilian Constitution stipulates that "there will be no penalties of a perpetual nature." Simply put, nobody in Brazil can be sentenced to life in prison. The Brazilian Penal Code, established when the life expectancy in Brazil was forty-three years old and not since updated, capped the maximum prison sentence that can be served by any individual at thirty years for all their crimes combined, regardless of the sentence they have been given. The thirty-year rule in Brazil ensures that, unless they die before their sentence concludes, all prison inmates will be released at some point. This rule also guarantees their frequent readmission because they emerge brutalized by their experiences, devoid of any employable skills, and largely ostracized by society. However, this rule is rarely invoked, as very few prisoners survive in the Brazilian prison system for even half that length of time before succumbing to disease or their fellow inmates.

Thus, Pedrinho Matador, sentenced to a cumulative 400 years, became eligible for parole in 2003.

Officially, Pedrinho was convicted of seventy-one murders, but he claimed responsibility for many more. In a 2003 article titled "A Monster of the System," journalist Ricardo Mondonca wrote, "He likes to embellish his reputation by sharing other stories, many of which we cannot verify whether they happened or not. Like many serial killers, his narratives often blur reality and fantasy, and most of the bodies he proudly claims to have dispatched were never found."

However, Mondonca continued to say that record-keeping in Brazilian prisons in the 1970s was "chaotic" and both authorities and journalists had to rely on oral testimonies to piece together certain homicide events. The article concluded, "Thus, it's likely that Pedrinho has killed fewer people than he claims, but more than his file indicates, showcasing the inefficiency of the police and the Judiciary."

The psychiatrists summoned to the prison to evaluate Pedrinho unanimously agreed: Killer Petey was a psychopath. He exhibited no remorse and no regret for his crimes. Indeed, he didn't even feign remorse, telling reporter Eduardo Faustini in 1996, "The things I do are good for society, in my opinion. I'm killing my enemies and people who rape, who kill children, who murder family men over a pair of sneakers... Do they deserve to live? Tell me! They don't."

Psychiatrist Antonio Jose Elias Andraus, one of the doctors who evaluated the serial killer, said, "Pedrinho is a cold psychopath who talks about deaths casually, without any remorse." However, the doctor conceded that most people did not need to fear him, saying, "You could enter the cell alone with him and he would never raise a hand. He spoke eloquently and appeared well-educated. To my knowledge, he never laid a hand on any staff member. But with the criminals, he dispensed his own form of justice. As he himself said, 'I could watch a person die and laugh. I felt nothing.'"

In the year leading up to his proposed release date, Pedrinho was transferred back to the State Penitentiary, where he behaved as an exemplary inmate. He assumed the role of cleaning coordinator and solemnly declared that he had no enemies and didn't plan on killing anyone. Unless he encountered the Park Maniac; him he would kill, just as he had promised.

Unaware that police, prison authorities, and politicians were convening to discuss possible actions regarding his case and whether they could legally keep him incarcerated, Pedrinho eagerly anticipated his release. He still looked youthful, thanks to his daily two-hour exercise regimen, and had a family to return to, despite them not visiting for several years. To make a living upon release, he figured he would return to working in a slaughterhouse, as he had done as a boy. He was the first to admit that he didn't know how to do anything else.

The Brazilian prison system didn't offer any type of rehabilitation programs. Recidivism rates for even regular prisoners were at least seventy percent, and Pedrinho had spent his entire adult life in prison. His colossal strength, amplified by his high adrenaline levels and absence of fear, made him a lethal weapon. And they had to let him loose in the world.

At the last minute, a judge unearthed a clause in the Criminal Code that could be construed to state that crimes committed after the commencement of a sentence could be regarded as new and separate. If interpreted this way,

Pedrinho's sentence could be extended to 2017. However, this interpretation could be contested in higher courts. Unfortunately for Pedrinho, he didn't have a lawyer and remained blissfully ignorant of the authorities' machinations to thwart his release.

When journalist Ricardo Mendonca visited him in the month of his proposed release, he found himself in the awkward position of seemingly knowing something Pedrinho didn't. He wrote, "He believes he will be released on the 25th. In reality, this will not occur. His sentence was extended due to the crimes he committed while incarcerated. Pedrinho could potentially appeal the decision, but he's unaware of it."

There's no record of how Pedrinho reacted to the news that his release would be delayed, but it was likely in the same stoic, impassive manner he exhibited when answering even the most invasive and impudent questions from interviewers over the years.

RELEASE

Someone must have helped Pedrinho appeal, because he was released from prison on April 24, 2007, after serving 34 years—four more than the law allowed. The Brazilian system does not monitor prisoners once released, so Pedrinho was left to fend for himself. He moved to a part of the country where he could evade the prying eyes of law enforcement. He settled in a pink cottage, surrounded by greenery, and acquired a labrador.

Adapting to the outside world took him a while. Everything was utterly foreign to him, and he had to ask for help for the simplest of tasks. He had no idea how to ride a train, buildings seemed to have sprung up out of nowhere, and the technology and machinery on farms were nothing like what he had seen before his incarceration. Television was now in color. Though he had seen plenty of mobile phones smuggled into the prison over the years, the internet was a mystery to him.

He led a quiet life, attending church in a village where most people knew the story of the man who claimed to have killed more than a hundred people and served thirty-four years in prison. He landed a job as a caretaker on a farm, and his neighbor later told reporters that Pedrinho was a hard-working, serious, and religious man.

There's not much to go on during this time, but it seems that the authorities had wanted to re-arrest Pedrinho almost from the moment he was released, but did not know where to find him. He was arrested on September 15, 2011, around 11 o'clock, in a farmhouse on the General Road of the Apes in Camboriú, following an anonymous tip-off to the Civil Police Division of Criminal Investigations.

Pedrinho was charged in relation to six riots he participated in while in prison and deprivation of liberty of a prison officer during one of those riots. Police also seized a loaded .38-caliber revolver that he wasn't supposed to possess, and he was charged with that too. He did not resist arrest and entrusted his labrador to his neighbor for care.

The media was waiting for him at the police station. He gave a press conference standing against the police banner where a dozen reporters thrust microphones at him. He calmly answered all their questions, many of which seemed designed to elicit sympathy for the killer.

"Do you think you've already paid for your crimes?" they asked.

Pedrinho nodded. "I've paid for my crimes," he said quietly.

Pedrinho fell back into the familiar routine of prison—working out, reading, and feeding his celebrity status. The fan mail came thicker and faster than ever, and news outlets sent a constant stream of reporters to interview him.

Inevitably, he was compared to Dexter, the serial killer in the TV series who only killed other killers. Like Dexter, Pedrinho claimed he was a vigilante, dispensing justice where the system had failed to do so and preventing further innocent deaths. He told reporter Roberto Cabrini: "I only killed those who were no good. If I didn't kill them, they would kill me, and they would kill others who didn't deserve to die."

In another prison interview in 2012, Marcelo Rezende asked him: "Is there anyone you kill that you regret killing, that you think maybe you shouldn't have?" Killer Petey answered that there was not. He didn't believe in regrets.

Thanks to the internet, the story of Killer Petey spread beyond Brazil. Pop-culture references to Dexter and the serial killer's unique but firm adherence to his own morals allowed people to support him. If you didn't look too closely and accepted the headlines at face value, this was a serial killer we could all get behind. He was The Punisher, the guy you needed when the only person who could properly deal with a bad guy was another bad guy. People conveniently forgot about the stories of those who were killed for the slightest and most mundane reasons. With his twisted logic, Killer Petey reasoned that if they were in prison, they were already guilty, so they deserved to die if he targeted them.

This time he had new visitors in addition to the constant procession of journalists—filmmakers who wanted to document his life, authors who wanted to help him write his biography, and people who wanted to be there when he got out to help him capitalize on his bizarre but undeniable celebrity status.

KILLER PETEY, SOCIAL MEDIA STAR

On December 6, 2017, Pedrinho Matador was once again released. At 64, he still looked youthful, thanks in part to his strict fitness regimen that started every morning at four o'clock. After making his bed, he would get straight into jumping rope, then onto stretching and holding the plank position for as long as he could. There were no more murder convictions in that time, although he told Roberto Cabrini of *Conexão Repórter* in an interview after his release that the last murder he carried out was "about five years ago." However, he also said it was outside, not inside prison, which would have placed it between 2007 and 2011. When pressed about that murder, Pedrinho didn't want to talk about it, saying: "It's kind of complicated, all right?"

In that same interview, Pedrinho also said he was done with killing unless someone were to harm his family. He remained close with his sister Clarice, his niece Jaqueline and her husband, catching up for regular family dinners. He desired a family of his own, a wife, a son and a daughter. He attended church regularly and was certain that God had forgiven his sins. He still had his enemies - a few months after his release, he was almost killed in Santa Catarina. Enemies were surprised to find him there, but with Killer Petey's reputation, they decided to go for reinforcements. By the time they returned, he had escaped to his sister's house. Pedrinho did not seek revenge. At least, that's what he said.

The world was still a foreign and crazy place to Pedrinho, but he came to embrace social media, where his story had taken on a life of its own. They called him the "Dexter Serial Killer," and his followers saw his crimes the way he did - that he was ridding the world of evil and protecting those who could not protect themselves. He became the vigilante many Brazilians believed they needed in a country where less than ten percent of murders are solved.

Pedrinho has amassed over 4,200 friends on Facebook, where he posts motivational quotes, videos of him showing off his culinary skills and pictures of his new tattoos. Piece by piece, he has been covering up the homemade and jail-house tattoos with professional artwork. He covered up his most infamous tattoo, the one that said "I kill for pleasure," with a picture of a scorpion. He covered up the tattoo that said "Revenge" with one that said "Love". The devil on his bicep was covered by a tribal tattoo. The wonky cross on his back became a picture of Jesus and cherubs. Maria's name was tattooed over by a feather. "I erased it because she no longer exists. She is no more," he told Roberto Cabrini. He lists himself on Facebook as "Single". The comments are filled with heart and flower emojis from female fans.

He has written and released the first part of his autobiography, which he sells through his social media platforms. Someone else has written a rap song about him. He's working on a documentary about his life with director

Bruno Santana. He's available for motivational talks and interviews.

He claimed that he wanted to leave Pedrinho Matador, "Killer Petey" behind. He told reporter William Cardoso, "I do not want to be known by that name anymore." But Killer Petey has become his brand. His YouTube channel, which has over 125,000 subscribers and more than eight million views, is called "Pedrinho Ex-Matador". His promo video is set to The Driving Force by the Jingle Punks, an uplifting soundtrack suggesting excitement and adventure. The wording lives up to the promise: "In this channel you will know and follow the life of the greatest serial killer in Brazil. Pedrinho Matador was sentenced to the largest penalty ever seen in Brazil. He beat the record for survival in jail and beat the record time arrested. There had never been another detainee spent so much time behind bars."

He is a prolific uploader, often adding several videos a day, sometimes live streaming. The videos are produced by thirty-year-old Pablo Silva. They are messages from Pedrinho about crime and God, archive footage of old interviews, reports on the sorts of crimes that he is morally opposed to, lessons for youth that crime doesn't pay, publicity for his book, and snippets of his day-to-day life: cooking, socializing, getting a haircut or a tattoo. He warns the kids of today that it is not just drugs that start trouble; things like vandalism, skateboarding, disrespecting older people and lying to parents about where they are going are all against his code of conduct.

He often gets stopped when he is out and about by fans keen for a selfie with the infamous killer. He is a genuine celebrity in his hometown. Nowadays when a policeman stops him on the street, it is to shake his hand and congratulate him. He is perhaps the first superstar serial killer.

Pedrinho Matador claims he craves the quiet life, living on a farm with a dog, surrounded by trees and animals. He sleeps through the night. He no longer has nightmares where the men he has killed return to him as animals that he must kill over and over again. He believes he is proof that psychopaths can be cured.

"In this world, where we are now... I'm not taking anyone's life... I'm cured," he told *Conexão Repórter* in 2019. The hour-long interview tried to find some degree of humanity and repentance in Pedrinho, but he remained emotionless throughout. It came across that this man was, indeed, a psychopath, who feels no remorse. It's like he wants to regret it but can't. He told the reporter: "I don't regret it because the people I killed weren't worth a shit. The people I murdered weren't even worth the food they eat. If I didn't kill them, they would kill me, they would kill other people who didn't deserve to die."

Cabrini asked: "Do you sometimes feel like a temptation, a will to kill?"

To which Killer Petey replied: "Yes, but it fades away."

EPILOGUE

On March 5, 2023, three years after this book was released, Pedro Rodrigues Filho, aka Killer Petey, was gunned down by two men in a drive-by shooting in front of his sister's house in Mogi das Cruzes. The murder occurred in broad daylight, at about 10:00 AM. To make sure he was dead, they slit his throat before fleeing in another car. A witness stated that one of the attackers was wearing a mask of the Joker character.

At the time of this update, no suspects had been arrested, but police had identified one man whom they believed to be responsible and who was on the run.

The legend of Killer Petey has survived his death, with one Brazilian newspaper saying, "Meanwhile, the eyes of Brazil turn to the big screen, in anticipation of seeing the life of this complex and controversial man depicted in a way never seen before. As the story of Pedro Rodrigues Filho continues to unfold, the country anxiously awaits the next chapters of this truly shocking plot."

PART III

SK CONFESSIONS

THE SELF-STYLED DEXTER SERIAL KILLER

A STRANGE SHOOT

On the morning of September 27, 2008, actor and comedian Chris Heward arrived at a two-car garage on a quiet street in suburban Edmonton, Canada, the location for his new film shoot. Chris had submitted his headshot and resume in response to an ad on Mandy.com to participate in a low-budget short thriller titled *House of Cards*. The actors weren't going to get paid, but the director claimed to be involved in a three-million-dollar major feature with Hollywood A-List actors and producers, promising to "remember things like work ethic and true acting chops when considering roles for that too."

The casting ad sought to fill numerous roles, but Chris felt qualified for the role of murder victim Roger, described as a "mid-40s family man type with a deceptive streak built from a place of insecurity."

Upon arrival, Chris was greeted by the director, a fresh-faced, dark-haired young man named Mark. The garage was set up for the murder scene, where Roger was lured to a remote location and killed, the footage intended for a snuff movie after responding to a profile on a dating website for cheating spouses. The script portrayed Roger as "your average working stiff who considers himself quite smooth at hiding things from his wife, but loses all his bravado when he's tied to a chair in a dark room revealing the wuss within."

The script set the scene:

Roger awakens with a splitting headache and a spell of dizziness. When his eyes adjust he takes stock of his situation. His hands are completely wrapped in duct tape and he is also fully duct-taped to a steel chair that is bolted to the floor. There is a strip of duct tape across his mouth. He's in an 8 foot by 24-foot storage area. A car is parked inside and there's a work table against the wall with a laptop on it. The laptop has superhero stickers on the back in a specific pattern. A person dressed in a large black PVC apron, with gloves and sporting a black street hockey mask with yellow streaks across it painted to look like a bear claw scratch with the mouth cut out suddenly appears out of nowhere, startling Roger.

The scene called for Roger to be killed with a samurai sword after being forced to provide all his computer passwords so the killer could empty his bank accounts.

Chris was taken aback to see that the weapons on the

table next to the chair he was to be tied to—including a stun baton, a butcher's knife, and a samurai sword—were not the plastic props he expected. As he sat in the chair with his arms and legs securely duct-taped, the director and the actor playing the murderer debated how to get the kill shot. The director suggested that the murderer charge at Chris and stab into the space beneath his armpit, making it look like he had been run through from the right camera angle. Chris wasn't comfortable doing this with a real sword and insisted a prop be used for the final lethal thrust.

As the cameras rolled, the script called for the killer to demand passwords from the gagged Roger. The actor growled, "Let's start with an easy one. What's your Cheating Hearts password?" As instructed, Chris strained and tried to speak, but couldn't make any intelligible noise due to the tape across his mouth. The script had laid out specific expectations for the actor playing the killer:

```
Killer: the actor needs to be able to
expertly  perform  through  a  mask
without getting corny or overdoing it.
I need cold, quiet and calm yet intim-
idating sociopath with a strong, even
tone voice.
```

Chris didn't have to dig too deep to act frightened for the scene. His unease was turning into a mild form of panic at the vulnerable position he was in. He hadn't told anybody where he was going to be. The director had been too quick to give him the part without an audition. The entire garage was soundproofed and windows were blacked out.

The actor playing the killer, wearing a black hockey mask painted with gold streaks, was thoroughly enjoying his role. He ripped the duct tape from Chris's lips and told him, "If you scream, I'm going to cut your windpipe out, which will cause a terrible mess and leave you unable to answer any more questions. So I'd advise you to restrain yourself."

The killer winds up and decapitates Roger in one smooth motion. The head slumps to the floor and as the neck spurts blood, the killer casually cleans the blade and puts it back into the scabbard, replacing it on the wall. He then picks up a power saw and goes to town on dismembering the body off screen. When we come back to seeing the killer, he's carefully packing the pieces into hefty bags and placing them in his trunk.

Chris breathed a sigh of relief when the tape was removed from his wrists and ankles. He helped them stuff his shirt with the filling from the cushions of an old couch. He was puzzled that for a scene requiring so much blood and carnage, they had forgotten to provide the fake blood. He figured they were more amateurish than he thought and realized he had no reason to be worried. The next day, he met the actresses who were to play his wife and daughter, finished filming preceding scenes in the home of the sound engineer, and before he knew it, his job was done.

Chris added *House of Cards*, the odd little indie film, to his resume and thought nothing more of it.

A SHOCK ENCOUNTER

EDITED TEXT:
A week later, on October 3, 2008, Marisa Girhiny and her boyfriend Trevor Hossinger were walking their dog near the same quiet street in suburban Edmonton when they came across a young, dark-haired man hunched over and staggering, with sweat pouring down his flushed face. As they approached, he stumbled into their path, collapsing before them. He had come from the direction of a nearby alleyway and was now thrashing about in what the couple thought was an overly dramatic manner.

The man was dressed in a torn dark shirt and had a large welt on his face. When he stood up, he was very unsteady on his feet, as if under the influence of drugs, and was screaming about someone trying to rob him. Before the couple could take it all in, another man emerged from the alleyway. This man was wearing a black and gold hockey mask and a hoodie, looking like a character out of a horror movie. The injured man cried out: "That's the guy!"

The masked man tapped the hockey mask as if to adjust

it and slipped behind a fence, peering over like a curious neighbor unwilling to miss any of the commotion unfolding on the street. Fearing they were being set up for a mugging, Marisa and Trevor began to back away. The masked man started to call out to the injured man, "Come on, Frank. Come back." His tone was light-hearted and friendly, but the entire situation made the couple extremely uneasy, and they made an about-turn, ready to head back toward home.

The unstable stranger cried out: "Can you at least help get me to my car?"

Trevor was torn between wanting to help the man and worrying he was being set up. The decision was made for him by Marisa, who was terrified by the man in the creepy mask still peeking over the fence at them, and the other man behaving so oddly in front of her. She began to shake uncontrollably, and Trevor knew he had to get his frightened girlfriend out of the situation as soon as possible. He put his arm around her and guided her away from the two men as quickly as he could.

When Marisa and Trevor got home, they called the police, who responded quickly. Returning to the spot in the alley, they could find nothing unusual. The police promised to keep an eye on the situation, but as the days passed without a report of a mugging from the injured man or any other crimes in the area, the couple decided it must have been a prank or an attempted opportunistic mugging that they had escaped.

They tried to put the terrifying incident out of their minds, but remained haunted by the memory of the panic in the injured man's eyes.

JOHNNY ALTINGER

Johnny Altinger was a typical bachelor in his thirties living in Edmonton during the early part of the twenty-first century. He owned a small apartment, which he was able to afford thanks to the modest profit he made from buying, renovating, and flipping a townhouse. He kept it quite neat and tidy if he expected visitors, but otherwise wouldn't bother making the bed. He worked as a pipeline worker, a job that he neither loved nor hated, but which provided a reasonable level of satisfaction. Despite residing in different cities, he maintained a close relationship with both his mother, Elfriede, and his older brother, Gary, as well as his tight-knit group of friends, some dating back to grade school.

Although Johnny had several hobbies, he was deeply passionate about his motorbikes and computers. Belonging to the first generation to grow up with a personal computer in the house, he convinced his mother to buy him a Commodore 64 when he was twelve. Since then, he consistently upgraded his systems through various iterations of hardware and software that hit the market, often being one of the early adopters. In the era of local bulletin board systems—the precursors to today's social media—Johnny dived in headfirst, making online friends who would eventually become friends in real life.

Friends and family described him as good-natured, light-hearted, generous, thoughtful, quiet, and affectionate. Though, as his mother noted, he wasn't blessed with the best looks, he was an optimistic, upbeat person. One friend said Johnny "tried to turn people's negative thoughts into positive ones." Recently, he had started exploring his spiritual side and joined a New Age group that dabbled in telepathy and astral travel. He also began taking clinical hypnotherapy classes. Weekends, if he wasn't out riding, might be spent playing paintball. He was a fan of Elton John.

By the time he was thirty-eight, Johnny had his life pretty well in order. He had family and friends who loved him, his own apartment, plenty of hobbies and interests, and a secure job working the night shift in quality control at Argus Machine, an oilfield equipment manufacturer. The only thing missing in his life was a partner to share it all with, something Johnny yearned for deeply. The escorts he occasionally hired from Craigslist didn't suffice.

Given his affinity and skill with computers, it was only natural that he would turn to internet dating. He hoped it would eventually lead him to a wife, or at least a companion he could enjoy life with in the interim. His preferred sites were two of the most popular free ones: PlentyOfFish.com and lavalife.com.

He went on several dates with different women, experiencing varying degrees of success, as could be expected from online match-making services. Some dates were enjoyable, but short-lived flings. Some matches didn't result in romantic relationships but evolved into friendships. And of course, there were the usual disasters, which he transformed into amusing anecdotes for his friends, taking the edge off the more awkward or painful encounters.

Johnny kept trying, maintaining his usual upbeat, positive approach, firmly believing that somewhere out there, the right girl was waiting for him.

A DATE WITH JEN

On the evening of October 10, 2008, Dale Smith received a phone call from his long-time friend, Johnny Altinger. The pair had known each other since elementary school, and conversations between them always flowed easily, meandering over a variety of topics, including Johnny's online dating adventures.

Johnny told Dale about an odd encounter he'd just experienced. Earlier, Johnny had forwarded Dale and another friend messages he'd received from a prospective date. He'd connected on PlentyOfFish with a woman named "Jen." They seemed like a good match: she was thirty-five, lived nearby, and her profile indicated she was looking for fun times, rather than a relationship. She was attractive and had posted a photo of herself in a bikini. Though Johnny knew such photos could be misleading, he was optimistic and excited for their planned date.

What seemed strange was that instead of providing an address, she sent detailed directions to a garage in an alley-way. She instructed him to enter through a partially open door. The drive was a ten-minute journey, over twenty-seven blocks. He'd shared these unusual instructions with his friends, who also agreed they were a bit odd.

Jen had written, "Although this sounds exciting, I have to make sure you're not some kind of weirdo. And so far, you seem to be fairly well put together, but anyone can lie online, right?" She explained that she would be able to see him before letting him into the house, a method for her to protect herself. Her message also hinted at the possibility of an extended stay:

> *Maybe this is paranoid on my part, but I have to look after myself, my first instincts about people and never wrong, and I know to trust them.*
>
> *I want to play very much, but I have to be cautious, as I'm sure you can understand. If you're okay with this, let me know. If not, we'll have to miss each other.*
>
> *On a lighter note, though, if we really get on, you said you had four days off. How long can I keep you for if I choose? Maybe you should pack for a few days. lol*
>
> *Jen.*

Dale had found the messages suspicious and suggested that Johnny call him once he arrived, to confirm he was safe.

It was after the date was supposed to have started when Johnny called with his latest tale of dating mishap. He shared that he'd arrived early, and upon reaching the garage, met a man who said Jen had lent him the garage to film movies. He even showed Johnny the props, including a fake gun, for a serial killer movie he was setting up. Jen had mentioned in one of her messages that she was letting a friend use the garage as a workspace over the weekend, so Johnny assumed this was the friend. Despite feigning interest in what the guy had to say, he was really there to meet Jen. However, the man told him that Jen was stuck in traffic and didn't know when she'd be home. Disappointed, Johnny went home, resigned to spending the night alone, and called Dale to share his story in his usual light-hearted manner.

Shortly after hanging up, Dale received another message from Johnny: "She's home now. I'm heading over again! HEHE"

Dale hoped his best friend would enjoy his date.

~

OVER THE WEEKEND, eager to hear about his friend's Friday night date, Dale left numerous messages for Johnny on voicemail and text. But Johnny didn't respond, which was out of character. Dale hoped the date had gone better than expected and that Johnny was simply too busy to reply.

By the time Thanksgiving Sunday arrived, Dale began to worry. Johnny had promised him a motorbike lesson and hadn't shown up nor called to explain his absence. Johnny owned two bikes—a Honda 500 cc and a Yamaha 1200 cc sport-touring bike—and loved riding them. Whenever he went away, he'd ask Dale to store them, rather than leaving them in his apartment's carport. Dale thought there was no one better to teach him how to ride.

It was typical of Johnny to share his passions with those he cared about. He often spent hours helping his less tech-savvy friends and family with computer issues. His brother, Gary Altinger, said, "Countless times he would sacrifice his own responsibilities to rescue me by word-processing term papers, essays, and other important assignments while I was attending university. I owe much of my academic success to John."

Friends often said that Johnny was so reliable, you could set your watch by him. So, it was completely out of character for him to not show up without an explanation. Dale continued to call and email, but there wasn't much else he could do. He hoped his friend was okay.

WHERE'S JOHNNY?

On Monday morning, Dale finally received an email from Johnny. It was cheerful and breezy, and it dropped a bombshell. It said: "I've met an extraordinary woman named Jen who has offered to take me on a nice, long tropical vacation. We'll be staying in her winter home in Costa Rica, phone number to follow soon. I won't be in town until December 10th but I will be checking my email periodically. John."

Dale was stunned. This did not sound like Johnny at all. Aside from the fact that Johnny always included a joke and never signed off with his name, preferring to finish with a wisecrack about his friend, he would never just blow off work to take an impromptu vacation. He was very diligent. Moreover, he had never liked warm holiday destinations. He went to Hawaii once and hated it. Lastly, Dale knew that, no matter what, if Johnny was going away, he would take a few minutes to call him, if only to ask him to store his bike while he was gone.

There was no doubt that the message had come from Johnny's email address, but Dale believed that his friend had not written those words. To test his theory, he sent a response, asking who would be picking up Johnny's brother at the airport when he came to visit. Johnny's brother wasn't actually coming, and Johnny would know this. Dale didn't get a response.

Deeply concerned, Dale began calling around to mutual friends and soon discovered others had received the exact same email. Each of them responded to Johnny, asking him to get in touch with them.

A previous online dating partner with whom Johnny had remained friends also found the strange email in her inbox. She was immediately suspicious as Johnny would invariably sign off with a joke or a smiley face, and always called her "sunshine." None of these hallmarks of her friend were contained in the email.

That same day, Johnny's Facebook status was updated to: "John is taking off to the Caribbean for a few months. See you all when I get back." Even more surprising to all who knew him, his relationship status was updated to "In a relationship".

That evening, Johnny's boss at Argus, Des Harte, received his unexpected resignation, via an email which said:

> Greetings. While I've certainly enjoyed my time at Argus, I have another offer that is just too good to pass up. So this is my notice that I will no longer be continuing my employment with your fine organization. I thank you for the opportunity and rest assured, I would not be leaving unless this new path I've chosen was truly life altering.
>
> Thank you, John Altinger

Des was extremely surprised. Johnny had worked at

Argus for over three years and was diligent and reliable. Nevertheless, he wrote back asking Johnny where to send his payout check, which amounted to almost $1,500.

A couple of days later, Johnny had still not responded to any of his friend's increasingly urgent emails. His boss wrote to him again, in a message that said:

John, There are many rumors floating around about what you have run off to do. All I need to know is where to forward your last check. Good luck in your endeavors wherever they may be.
Regards, Des Harte

Johnny didn't respond to any of the email messages, but his MSN Messenger status was changed to "I've got a one-way ticket to heaven, and I'm never coming back". Meanwhile, his Facebook status was updated once more, to say: "John is wondering why anyone would leave sun and surf to come home to snow and stress".

To those who knew him, none of this was adding up. Johnny Altinger hated hot weather. He was also by no means wealthy and would have needed that final pay check. But most of all, he was in constant communication with his friends and would never have left them hanging when he knew they were worried.

Carrie-Lynn Souza, the wife of one of Johnny's friends, who had never met him but had become concerned as her husband and his mates tried to get hold of their friend, decided to send him a Facebook message, which said: "Hi John, please respond as soon as you get this, or at least call Dale. Everyone is concerned for you. Thanks, Carrie-Lynn."

To everybody's surprise, even though he had apparently ignored messages from his closest friends, Johnny responded promptly to Carrie-Lynn. His message said: "Hi

Carrie. No need to be worried. I'm on vacation and loving it. The internet is much easier to use than phones, due to terrible reception and cost. I just need to get away for a while, and I'm with someone wonderful. I'll try to get in touch with Dale as soon as possible. But in the meantime, let him know I'm having the time of my life."

Carrie-Lynn passed the message on, but the fact that Johnny had responded to a woman who was a virtual stranger while ignoring the messages from his closest friends fueled their suspicions that something had gone horribly wrong and whoever was sending the messages, it wasn't Johnny Altinger. Carrie-Lynn responded to the message telling him he should respect the fact that he had some very good friends, and that due to their concern, email at this point was unsatisfactory. She provided him with a number that he could call collect and warned him if he hadn't called by 6:30 p.m., they would be following up with the Edmonton City Police.

When the response never came, the group of friends followed through by contacting the police to make a missing person's report. The police didn't seem particularly interested. After all, there was a perfectly good explanation provided directly from the accounts of the missing man himself – he had gone on a fabulous holiday with a gorgeous woman he had met online. His friends agreed that the messages came from Johnny's own email and Facebook accounts. There was no reason for the police to think Johnny was in danger. The most obvious answer was that Johnny was lying on a beach somewhere, with his cell phone turned off and not thinking about his buddies at all.

Although this was objectively reasonable from the point of view of the police, Johnny's friends were certain something was wrong. They decided there was only one thing they could do - break into Johnny's apartment and see if there were any clues to his sudden departure there.

As the friends arrived at the four-story apricot condominium block at 11445 Ellerslie Road, a short drive from his work at Argus Machine, they didn't even have to go inside to have their initial fears compounded. Johnny's beloved motorcycle was in the outdoor parking lot of the complex, uncovered. They knew he wouldn't have left it like that. His red Mazda, on the other hand, was missing.

Proceeding inside, they broke a window to gain access to Johnny's apartment. The bachelor pad was familiar to them all and the mess that greeted them was not cause for specific alarm, as Johnny was a fairly typical single gamer guy in that respect. The mess did tell them, however, that he had not expected to bring home any female company that night. Dishes were left unwashed in the sink, his paintball gun was on his unmade bed, not yet having been put away from the most recent game. A CD case lay open on the white leather couch that dominated his lounge room. His motorcycle jacket hung casually over the back of a kitchen chair, and his helmet had been left on the table. Everything pointed to a man who had gone out but would be returning home shortly.

His laptop was missing and so, strangely, was his printer. The clincher was what they found in his desk drawer. Johnny's passport. He could not have gone to Costa Rica without it.

When the friends returned to the Edmonton police with the evidence they had found, they insisted that their concerns be taken seriously, which to their credit, the Edmonton police did. Detective Bill Clark opened a missing persons file on Friday, October 17, 2008, one week after the last confirmed communication with Johnny Altinger.

FOLLOWING LEADS

The friends handed over the strange emails and Facebook messages, Johnny's passport, and all the information they thought might be relevant to Detective Clark. A search of the international airport's parking lot revealed that the red Mazda wasn't there, another clue that Johnny had not left the country. Police combed through the passenger lists of all the airlines that flew out of the international airport, and Johnny's name wasn't on any of them. It seemed that his friends might be on the right track. Wherever Johnny was, he hadn't left the country via the airport.

By far the strongest clue the police had was the detailed instructions provided to Johnny by "Jen" for their date. Detective Clark was surprised Johnny had forwarded those instructions to two friends before going out. There are constant warnings to women on dating sites to exercise caution, meet in a public place, and always let somebody know where you are going and when you expected to be home, but it was far less common for men to do so. Dale

Smith recalled Johnny saying something like: "If anything happens to me, you'll know where to look."

The emails did not contain a street address, but rather explicit turn-by-turn instructions:

> Ok if you're coming from the South, best thing to do is to use the Whitemud to get to 50 st and go south. Then you go right on 40 ave and after a couple blocks turn right again at a yellow cross-walk sign in to the alley. Some guy parks his RV there so pay attention lol.
>
> Once you do that, just go left and park in the only driveway on your left that looks like a forest, lol. What did I say? fixer upper . . . yeah not paved. There's a couch and some other garbage I haven't had time to call the city about yet. I'll just leave the garage door partly open for you to sneak in through. Just make sure you push the button at the regular door to close the big door. I have a friend coming over to use part of it as a workshop this weekend so he blanketed off where my car usually goes lol.
>
> Like I need red spray paint on my car right, don't ask.
>
> I'm going to be out and about today because my gf just called me and got me into hanging out with her but you and I can get together at 7:00. I'll be back by then.
>
> Sound good?

The directions led detectives to a garage in a laneway in Mill Woods, a quiet suburban area, at which they arrived late, close to midnight. It was locked with a combination padlock. The windows all appeared to be covered up, but one of the constables peeked through a small hole and could see that there was a light on in the garage. It appeared clean and there was no one inside, as far as the officer could see.

The constables knocked on the door of the house, but there was no answer. They decided to apply for a search warrant first thing the next day to enter the garage. In the meantime, they kept a lookout for the red Mazda and started covering other avenues, such as trying to get in touch with Johnny's family.

The request for a search warrant was denied as there was no evidence any crime had been committed. However, their inquiries led the police to Kirkside Real Estate, who confirmed they had rented out the garage to an independent filmmaker who had been using the space to shoot a short film.

That evening, Constable Maxwell called Mark Twitchell at his home in St. Albert to tell him there was a problem with the garage he was renting. The director readily agreed to come and open up the garage, despite it being some distance away and late at night.

At around 11:30 pm on October 18, nearly nine days after Johnny Altinger's disappearance, a maroon-colored Grand AM sedan pulled up outside the garage. The baby-faced dark-haired man introduced himself as Mark Twitchell. He was ruffled, having had to pull over twice on the way to answer urgent calls from Kirkland Real Estate, from which he surmised that someone had been using the garage on certain nights without his knowledge, perhaps having a party, and had left the lights on.

Mark went to let the police into the garage but expressed surprise at the lock, which he said was not the same padlock he'd been using. His was silver on the outside with a black plastic dial in the center, but the one they were faced with now was pure metal and Mark said he didn't know the combination to it. He readily agreed to let the police officers break the lock, which they did easily by simply unscrewing the latch that held it.

Mark explained that he rented the garage for $175 a month. The upstairs area of the house on the same property was rented to a group of temporary foreign workers, while someone else lived in the basement. Mark didn't have any contact with the other people in the house.

Constable Maxwell went in first. The first thing he noticed was the strong smell of something having been recently burned. It emanated from an oil drum in one corner, which was discolored in places as though it had been scorched. Opening the lid, Maxwell could see the charred remains of something inside.

Mark Twitchell looked shocked at the state of the barrel. He said he had it delivered to be used as a garbage can and it hadn't been scorched when he had last seen it. The officers also noted a few red spatters, and Mark explained that he had used the space to film a scene in his short psychological thriller, *House of Cards*, in late September. The spatters were most likely the fake blood from the scene. Mark said he noticed several things out of place, suggesting someone else had been there. Most of his roll of duct tape had been used, all his garbage bags were gone, and the unopened bottle of cleaner now appeared half empty.

The constable noted that the windows were all blocked, and once the roller doors were closed, it was nearly impossible to see in. Mark explained that it was important that the lights could be blocked out so that during the day when filming a nighttime scene, the sunlight wouldn't interfere.

The officers decided to call their staff sergeant, and while waiting, Constable Maxwell and Mark Twitchell chatted in the front seat of the police car, while Mark completed a written statement. It was a pleasant conversation, mostly centered on Mark's filmmaking and interest in Star Wars. Mark told the constable that he was happily married with a baby girl. When he was asked if he would be willing to come back to the station to answer some questions, Mark once again readily agreed.

QUESTIONS FOR THE DIRECTOR

It was around 3:30 a.m. when Detective Mike Tabler began to interview Mark at the local police station. Mark was forthcoming and helpful, although he seemed more keen to talk about his movies than a missing person. He explained that *House of Cards* was a short film of eight or nine minutes that was to be submitted to film festivals in the hope of getting noticed by investors who would fund a full-length feature film. He also planned to use it in a reel as pitch material in the hopes of developing a television series. He regaled the detective with details of the feature film, a comedy, he was working on and said that he had lined up A-list actors and a co-producer in LA who had worked on *Ocean's Eleven*.

Detective Tabler gently steered him back to more relevant topics, such as the names of all the people who had worked on *House of Cards* and who had been in the garage or had access to it. Mark readily provided all such details to him and told him the last time he had been in the garage was Friday, October 10th. Detective Tabler knew that was the same day as the last confirmed contact Johnny Altinger's friends had had with him, but he didn't let that on to Mark.

Mark told the detective about the scene of the man in the chair and described how the production crew had made up large quantities of fake blood using corn syrup and food dye, which looked very realistic and was messy as hell.

Detective Tabler pointed out that it was an odd coincidence that he was filming a serial killer movie and that the police had been called to that garage because of a missing person who supposedly had gone there. Mark agreed with him vigorously, saying, "I got this weird chill, 'cause it just doesn't sit right. So the first thing I start asking myself is who all knows about what we do there and what our schedule looks like?"

Mark provided a list of people who had access to the garage that he knew of, their names, ages, jobs on the set, and phone numbers. When Detective Tabler asked him if he knew of someone by the name of Johnny Altinger, Mark was positive he had never heard the name. He wasn't an actor or in any way connected with *House of Cards*, as far as Mark knew. The detective provided him with more details about Johnny's last known activity, which led to the garage where he had encountered a man. Mark appeared baffled by the entire scenario. He claimed to know nobody by the name of Jen. The only dating sites he knew of were those he had looked into for the purposes of writing a freelance article a month previously.

The interview lasted a long time, and Mark Twitchell seemed eager to help. The rudimentary background check that had been done when they first learned of him revealed that he came from a good home and there had been no history of violence or criminality, although there was an old bankruptcy that would soon be discharged. Eventually, they sent the exhausted young director home, with instructions that he should let the police know if he recalled anything else that may help them find the missing Johnny Altinger.

STRANGE EVENTS

They didn't have to wait long. The next day, Detective Tabler received a three-page email from Mark Twitchell. In it, Mark claimed that when he had arrived home after 5:00 a.m., tired and overwhelmed, he had filled his wife in on what had transpired that evening, and she reminded him of a couple of other strange events that had happened recently. Mark thought they might be related.

The first had happened a few days earlier, on a Wednesday. He had just pulled over to answer a phone call after getting gas when a stranger had knocked on his car window. He recalled the man as being around 6'2", medium build, Caucasian with black medium-length hair. Assuming the man was going to ask for either money or directions, Mark rolled down his window and was surprised instead when the man asked if he would like to buy his car, a red Mazda 323, offering to sell it to Mark for whatever cash he had on him. Jokingly, Mark told him he had only forty dollars and was surprised when the man readily agreed to sell it to him for that amount of money.

The man told him he had hooked up with a sugar momma who was going to give him a brand-new BMW, so he no longer needed the Mazda. He just wanted to get rid of it before taking off on an all-expenses-paid vacation. Mark was suspicious but figured that at worst, he would be out forty dollars, and at best, he would have a reasonable-looking car. He agreed to let the man follow him to the garage.

When they arrived, Mark said, "his even-keeled disposition all but disappeared when we got to the garage, and I was getting a weird vibe from him." The man seemed to want to get going quickly but showed him what appeared to be genuine registration and insurance and then took off.

When Mark realized that the Mazda had a manual transmission, which he didn't know how to drive, he had his friend Joss collect the car and park it in his garage for a while. Joss had worked on *House of Cards*, but Mark had forgotten to mention him the day before because he was a quiet guy without a specific role. He had helped design Mark's website.

Mark also wrote that his wife had reminded him of another incident that had happened the previous week. His car had been broken into while he was at a show with Joss. He didn't have much of value in there, but they had taken a pair of sunglasses, loose cash out of the cup holder, and a bunch of receipts, including a Western Union receipt with his home address on it and two receipts for the rent of the garage with the garage's address on them.

Then, on Thanksgiving Sunday, upon returning home from dinner at the in-laws', the couple noticed that the front door of their house was unlocked. Mark searched the house carefully as his wife Jess held onto their baby daughter, but they didn't notice anything missing or any signs of an intruder. They chalked it up to paranoia and fatigue.

He finished up the email writing:

I don't mind saying this is all seriously stressing me out. Identity theft is the first concern, my home being compromised is now another one and we're strongly considering getting an active security system installed next week. I feel violated and angry that anyone was rooting around in my personal stuff without my knowledge and now I'm greatly worried that they likely know where I live. My car has a distinctive appearance and an easily identifiable custom plate and I'm wondering if this fellow who pawned the car off on me had seen mine before and might have been waiting for me or following me. I just don't know any more. He could have been the person who broke into my car as well. There's a hundred different scenarios rushing through my mind right now and I'm not a fan of any of them.

Detective Tabler showed the strange email to his colleagues. At this point, they weren't even sure that Johnny Altinger was genuinely missing, but with the absurd story about the purchase of a car from a stranger for forty dollars, they decided it was time to take a closer look at Mark Twitchell.

MARK TWITCHELL

Twenty-nine-year-old Mark Andrew Twitchell lived with his wife, Jess, and their baby daughter, Chloe, in a home they had bought the previous year. Jess had insisted on the move to Edmonton once she had become pregnant because she hated everything about their previous place. She hated the heat, the smell, the layout, the neighborhood, and she made it very clear to Mark that they needed to get a real house in a nice area. She threatened him that the living situation would continue to put such a strain on the marriage that it might not last. Mark did what he had to do, got a mortgage, and the couple moved into the split-level home behind the white picket fence.

Jess was Mark's second wife, the couple having met through an online dating service and married in 2006. However, by 2008, their marriage was already on the rocks, and they were sleeping in separate bedrooms. Nevertheless, Mark claimed that Jess was a wonderful mother to their eight-month-old daughter, with whom he was besotted. He believed his little girl to be exceptionally adorable and denied this was mere parental pride, as it was something that other people were quick to tell him as well.

Jess was not happy with the amount of time Mark spent on his filmmaking, which brought in little money. Mark had always loved films and was a regular cosplayer, dressing up in various costumes to attend sci-fi and fantasy conventions, where he liked to get photos with the stars of his favorite shows. His custom-made dress-ups were elaborate and included characters like Wolverine, Predator, nearly every major Star Wars character, and a spectacular Bumblebee Transformer costume, which won him over $3,000 in prizes at Halloween contests put on by radio stations. He later sold the costume for "a substantial amount." If there was an excuse to dress up, Mark was there and gave it his all. Halloween was his Christmas.

But all this came at the expense of spending time and money on his family, so at Jess's insistence, they started attending couples therapy. Mark also agreed to attend weekly one-on-one counseling sessions with a psychiatrist every Friday night. He dutifully filled Jess in on the details of each meeting, and it seemed like the appointments were helping. It was important that they tried to keep their marriage together for their little girl.

❧

ON OCTOBER 20, Mark Twitchell attended the Edmonton Police Services Headquarters, where he was interviewed by Bill Clark, a detective skilled in the art of grilling major suspects. Clark had been on the force for over 30 years and risen to be the force's star interrogator. His style was a throwback to earlier days of police investigations. Some of the younger guys ribbed him about his old-school ways and jokingly called him "Sipowitz" after the hard-nosed cop on TV crime drama NYPD Blues. There was nothing Clark liked better than to sink his teeth into a juicy case, and when he found an inconsistency in testimony or a weakness in a suspect, he would grab hold and not let go. He called himself a pit bull.

When Detective Clark entered the room, Mark was sitting comfortably on a small couch beneath a framed landscape painting. Clark reminded him that he was welcome to call a lawyer if he wanted to. Mark acknowledged the offer but deemed it unnecessary.

Detective Clark started by saying, "Right now, I don't know if I'm investigating a crime or I'm just investigating a missing person." He asked Mark to tell him everything from the beginning. This was a much longer interview than his previous one, with the veteran detective probing every facet of Mark's story. He asked about the clean-up of the fake blood and what exactly seemed to have been missing or messed up when Mark entered with the detectives after they broke the lock. They went through all the relevant days and events, trying to jog Mark's memory or bring out more details about people who had been in the garage or might have had access. Mark confirmed that two of his film crew knew the combination of the padlock that had previously been used on the garage before the mystery lock appeared.

Mark told him that on the day of the strange car sale, he had filled a jerry can with fuel for a lawnmower he had planned to buy. The can was still in the trunk of his car, but he had used half of it to fill his tank since then. He recalled the extra detail that the sketchy seller had a Celtic knot tattooed on his neck, about three inches in diameter.

After more than an hour and a half of grilling about Mark's recollections and movements, Detective Bill Clark suddenly switched gear and changed the line of questioning. He shot out questions like:

"So Mark, what do you think happened to this John Altinger guy?"

"Do you think somebody has done something to harm him?"

"Do you think he's really missing?"

"How do you think the results of this investigation are gonna come out on you?"

To each of these questions, Mark answered that he didn't know, although to the last he said, "Well, positively I would think. I've been trying to tell you guys everything that I know."

Detective Clark kept on at him: "What do you think should happen to the person if there's been harm done to John Altinger? What if we find out there's been foul play and he's been murdered? What do you think should happen to the person? Do you think if there's been foul play to John that the person who did this to him deserves a second chance under any circumstances?"

Mark responded that the person should go to prison with no mercy.

Finally, Clark asked, "Mark, did you have any involvement in the disappearance of John?" And when he responded "no," the detective kept at him: "None whatsoever? Absolutely positive on that?"

Each time, Mark Twitchell answered calmly, "No."

At the 2-and-a-half-hour point, after leaving the room for a little while and then returning, Detective Clark's demeanor had changed again. He said, "Mark, you remember I mentioned to you earlier about contacting a lawyer? That still holds true, okay, just so you're aware. If at any time we're talking, you wanna contact a lawyer, you can do so at any time. I'll take you to a phone. There's something else I wanna tell you, Mark, and that's that there's absolutely no doubt in my mind that you're involved in the disappearance of John Altinger. No doubt in my mind at all, Mark."

Bill Clark had firmly switched to the role of Bad Cop, a role he relished, and now his accusations were relentless and aggressive. Mark was rattled but continued to deny any involvement. The detective told him that other detectives had been talking to his neighbors and had called Joss—the friend to whom Mark had passed on the car—while Mark was being interrogated. Clark accused him of lying about the lock, telling him that the neighbors had seen Mark change the lock on the garage a week and a half earlier. Clark said to him:

"So that's a lie, that's a lie you told me. When you gave your version of events to Detective Tabler last night, your version of events was different than what you told me today. What you wrote down was different than what you told me in this room. What you told me in this room when I first came in was different from your final version of events. You've changed your whole story. All kinds of different lies. Now I know this isn't an easy thing to live with. Somethin' went wrong there. Like I said I don't think you're a bad guy, you seem like a decent guy. You gotta wife. You gotta small child. You're tryin' to do the best. I don't know, but I don't think you're doin' that well financially. I think it's a tough life what you're in. You're trying to do your best but something went wrong. Maybe you were just trying to make a better movie, I don't know. But something went wrong and you're involved. And this is not gonna go away Mark. And you know that you're not a dumb guy. You know it's not gonna go away. This is gonna keep on eatin' at you and eatin' at you."

He went on to pick holes in the conflicting stories that Mark had come up with thus far: "You are definitely not a dumb man. You know very well that you don't buy a car that's worth over ten thousand dollars from someone for forty dollars. ... Your reason for having gas doesn't even make sense. You're buyin' gas for a lawnmower you don't own. You're buyin' gas just to keep in your car. No. You're buyin' gas to get rid of things. You shake your head, but you know what I'm sayin' is true."

The detective hammered away at him, reminding him he told the original police who turned up that he hadn't seen a red car in the area, somehow forgetting that he had bought a car matching that description for forty dollars just a couple of days earlier. The barrel he had bought to act as a rubbish bin was known as a "burn barrel" in the industry. Mark had the missing man's license plates and his keys.

But Mark wasn't budging. Sick of the hammering he was getting, he finally demanded to know if he was free to go. With no hard evidence, Clark was forced to let him leave. But as Mark got up, the detective told him his car was being seized, and they were getting a search warrant to go through it, and anything suspicious would be sent off to forensics.

Mark shrugged and nodded. The detective had another parting shot: "It's gonna eat at you. If you're a normal person, it's gonna eat at you."

But Mark knew it would not eat at him too much. He told the detective, "You'd be surprised what I can live with."

GATHERING EVIDENCE

Following his hours-long grilling by Bill Clark, Mark Twitchell engaged a lawyer, and that was it for interrogations. The detectives on the case had no doubt that whatever had happened to Johnny Altinger, Mark had something to do with it.

But what had happened to Johnny? They still didn't know if they were looking at a missing person's case or something far more sinister.

They had enough now to obtain search warrants, and on October 21, they were granted permission to search Mark's Grand AM, Johnny's Mazda, Mark's home in St. Albert, and the garage studio in Mill Woods.

The next day, they got a fifth warrant for Mark's cell phone, which allowed them to monitor incoming and outgoing calls. It also provided cell tower information, giving the police an approximate location whenever the phone was used.

The police started combing through the evidence they had so far. His maroon Pontiac Grand Am, which bore the vanity plates DRK JEDI, revealed evidence that further cemented the detectives' view that Mark knew what happened to Johnny. In the trunk, they found a half-empty gas can and bloodstains in the interior fabric, which were sent off for forensic testing. Also sent to forensics was the Toshiba laptop that they had found inside the car, which was covered in superhero stickers, some of which appeared to be stained with blood. They noted that Mark kept a paperback copy of one of the Dexter novels in his back seat.

Other items recovered from Mark's car included a hunting knife with what appeared to be blood on it and post-its with cryptic handwritten notes on them that included, among other instructions: "Ship phone while it's on," "return addy of vic," "destroy wallet contents," and "kill room clean sweep." Then there were the roughly-drawn maps, including one of a path from St. Albert, where Mark lived, to the crossroads near Johnny's condo.

Bill Clark's hunch was now a certainty, but everything they had was circumstantial and could be explained away by a clever lawyer. Their number one priority was finding Johnny Altinger, dead or alive.

They took swabs from several items in Johnny's apartment, including cutlery, nail clippers, a razor, drinking straws, and glasses, all of which were sent off to the lab for comparison testing on items found in Mark's garage.

They looked into any other suspicious incidents that had happened in the vicinity of the garage and came across a strange police report that had been made a few weeks earlier. A couple had been out walking their dog when a man fell into their path, begging them to help him. When another man appeared wearing a hoodie and a hockey mask, the couple freaked out, thinking they were being set up for a mugging and hurried away. They called the police upon returning home and returned to the area, which was right near the garage. Several squad members accompanied them, but they found nothing of concern.

Nobody had ever come forward that matched the description of the man, and there were no reports of a robbery in the area. Detectives on the case immediately wondered if the couple had encountered Johnny Altinger, but the dates didn't make sense. The report was filed a week before Johnny went missing. They added the incident to the rapidly growing case file.

They started the tedious job of tracking down and making appointments to speak to all the people who had worked on films with Mark in that garage.

Some of the people in Mark's circle planted seeds of doubt, suggesting that the young filmmaker was pulling a publicity stunt. He was known to be passionate about his film career and willing to do anything to get noticed. The whole thing could be a hoax designed to promote his films.

Others mentioned an email that Mark had circulated among friends and colleagues, which suggested they should not talk to the police, whom Mark accused of fabricating evidence. He wrote to his friends:

I have to recommend everybody stop talking to the police or not to start if you haven't already. You all have a right to silence and you should exercise that right. I'm sure no one in this group carries guilt so you have nothing to fear, but I've been screwed around with and don't appreciate it, so it's time to stop this and make them do their own jobs. Sometimes what we see on TV is in fact a true representation of how they work. Sometimes they do lie and make things up in order to make you say things they otherwise would not just so they could have an answer for the media. I'm serious. The time for dry, sarcastic humour and flaky jokes is over and this is no prank.

The garage was marked as a crime scene, which forensic specialists went over with luminol. The chemical revealed a large patch on the floor and several spatters on the wall of what they suspected was blood. Police seized the cleaning supplies that Mark had admitted to buying a few days earlier but denied having used. The ammonia bottle was marked in spots with what appeared to be blood. The game processing kit consisting of several knives and tools such as a rib-spreading tool would no doubt be explained away by Mark as props for his serial killer movie. Forensics would determine whether the red stains on the tools were real blood or the corn syrup and food dye mixture. Another interesting item was a metal pipe wrapped on one end in black cloth tape. Blood and tissue appeared to be embedded in the thread of the pipe on the other end.

With the evidence pointing to him mounting rapidly, police set up a surveillance team to watch Mark Twitchell around the clock, but nothing in his behavior aroused suspicion. And dig as they might, they could find no motive for Mark to have killed Johnny Altinger. There was nothing to suggest the two men knew each other. Neither man had any sort of criminal history. Mark Twitchell was an ordinary man with a wife and child and a passion for movies. Why would he kill a perfect stranger?

That was the most perplexing question of all, and one that the detectives struggled to find an explanation for. It seemed to be a dead end until they got a call from the forensic computer specialist who had examined the laptop that had been left in Mark Twitchell's car. The computer forensics team was able to restore a file that had been deleted from Mark Twitchell's computer. It was a text file called *SK Confessions*.

The file was a document that ran to over forty pages. The

introduction said: "This story is based on true events. The names and events were altered slightly to protect the guilty." As Mark Anstey, the primary investigator in charge of solving Johnny's disappearance, read through the file, his blood ran cold.

He was in no doubt that "SK" stood for "serial killer," and what he was reading was a first-person account of the murder and dismemberment of Johnny Altinger.

SK CONFESSIONS

T he recovered file was written in the form of a story
written to read like a diary. The opening paragraph read:

*This is the story of my progression
into becoming a serial killer. Like
anyone just starting out in a new
skill, I had a bit of trial and error
in the beginning of my misadventures.
Allow me to start from the beginning
and I think you'll see what I mean.*

The story first went into the background of its author,
saying he had always known he was different when he realized other people had emotions like empathy, which he
could not relate to. He said he had become an expert at
covering his true nature, lying to say what he thought others
wanted to hear, while always harboring dark fantasies.

In the story, the author had resolved that he wanted to
make his first kill of what would become many by the time

he was thirty. But first, he had to educate himself, reading up on mistakes others made, determined he would not make the same. Then he started to plan out just whom he would target and how he would kill them and get away with it. He settled on single men in their thirties looking for love. He wrote:

> I would use online dating to rope in my victims. Once I came up with that one clear starting point, all of the other pieces needed to be tended to. I began to ask myself a series of questions designed to get me to consider every possible angle. I wanted to have every step in the process already planned out from start to finish because improvising would be bad and lead to sloppiness. I had to have an order, a plan, something that would bring calm to a chaotic situation.

He wrote that he wanted not just to kill and get away with it, but he would figure out ways to profit from each of the murders. He described finding the perfect location to carry out his murders:

> A double detached garage for rent in the south of the city, tucked away in a quiet neighborhood on a lot with a house occupied by tenants who couldn't even read English, much less speak it.

Paragraph after paragraph described the preparations

made to the garage, shopping lists of essential items, and practice with the tools of his new trade. He wrote of his excitement at finding a hunter's game processing kit, designed to take apart large mammals, which would reduce the blood spatter inevitably caused by power tools. He wanted his kill knife to be "simple, elegant, and beautiful" and chose "a well-crafted hunting knife with an 8-inch blade" that he found at a military surplus store.

Once everything was perfect in what he called his "little workshop of horrors", the would-be killer set about creating new internet identities, first downloading an IP blocker so that no internet traffic would be traced back to him and generating dozens of random email addresses. Once he set up profiles on dating sites, all he had to do was sit back and wait for the offers to come rolling in from lonely, horny men.

He decided his kill days would fall on Fridays, the evening he had a fake appointment with an imaginary psychiatrist and wouldn't be expected home by his wife. He wrote:

> *Starting a kill on a Friday works on so many levels. For one thing, most people are not hard and fast expected to be anywhere on the weekend which gives me three days to clean up and tie up the loose ends.*

When it came time for the kill, the story described luring in a man who fit the profile, then almost letting him go again when he turned up early and caught the killer in the garage, still preparing. When the man came back a second time, the killer had lost his nerve and told him that his date was stuck in traffic. It was only when the victim messaged his date again, still keen to get together, that the killer invited him back, and this time had his trap set.

The detectives on the Johnny Altinger case read through the story in stunned disbelief. Every single part of it matched up to evidence they had already found or already knew. The garage and all the items in it were identical. Crucially, parts of the story matched up to information Mark Twitchell could not have known if he was not the killer, such as the victim turning up early and talking to a man in the garage, who showed him the theatrical props, just as Johnny had told his friend Dale that fateful Friday evening. Reading on, they knew they were about to find out just what happened to Johnny when he returned to that garage after shooting off one last joyous email to Dale that said: 'She's home now. I'm heading over again! HEHE.'

SK Confessions then went into gleeful, gory detail of the next few hours. It described the efforts by the man, who is called 'Jim' in SK Confessions but who police were positive was Johnny, to get away, followed by his murder, dismemberment, and then cleanup afterward.

The story went into minute detail. One passage spoke of the killer trying to burn his victim's remains in a barrel, just like the one police found inside the garage with gas from a jerry can, just like the half-empty one in the trunk of his car.

The names of the killer's family were wife Tess and infant Zoe. Mark's wife was Jess, his daughter Chloe. In the story, the killer's wife called just after he had finished dismembering the victim to ask where he was:

```
My phone rang. The familiar buzzing of
its vibrate setting going off. The
caller ID showed it was Tess calling.
What could I do? I answered.
```

"Hi baby, what's up?"

"Not much. Where are you?"

"I'm just leaving the gym hun."

"The gym closes at nine."

I checked my watch hurriedly, it showed 9:57 pm. My mind raced. I couldn't get caught in a lie. Not again.

"What are you talking about babe? It closes at ten."

"The big gym by our place?"

And there was my window. I had switched gyms when we moved to our new house so it sorted itself out as I jumped back in to play the game. "No, my old gym babe".

"I thought you canceled the membership a month ago."

"I procrastinated . . . " as I do tend to do quite often. "And did it a few weeks ago but I still have a couple weeks this month that are paid for so I figured I'd take advantage since it takes an hour to cross town anyway."

The story finished up with the killer using the keys he'd stolen to break into the victim's apartment, which he described as being exactly like Johnny's. He took the cash he found in the dresser, the laptop and printer, and a few other pieces of interest. The killer fired up his victim's computer and found to his delight that Johnny stayed logged in to all of his email and social media accounts. He wrote:

I couldn't have had an easier time. I
changed the auto response on his email
to say he had decided to run away with
the woman he hooked up with on Friday
to go on a two month vacation to the
Caribbean.

Unfortunately for the police, the story ended before it
got to the part that described what the killer had done with
Johnny's body. However, assuming it was a factual account, it
had given them many further details they could check.

One of those details was that Johnny Altinger might not
have been the killer's first victim.

A VISIT WITH JESS

On October 24, detectives paid a visit to the home that Mark shared with his wife and daughter. They confiscated a number of items, including swords kept in various corners, a box for an electronic stun gun, sales receipts for a butcher knife and handcuffs, an air pistol with baby blue pellets, draft designs for a metal chair and table, and a large black, old-style goalie mask, with three gold stripes painted along its face and a cutout chin. The mask was in the basement that Mark used as an office, on a pile of clothes near his computer, which they also seized. In his room, they found blue jeans and a sweatshirt with what appeared to be bloodstains, and burned Season 2 Dexter DVDs.

In discussions with Mark's wife Jess, police discovered the marriage had been troubled lately and Mark was sleeping in the basement. Jess was increasingly convinced that Mark was gaslighting her. She knew he was having an affair with an ex-girlfriend, but Jess was confident that he had been unfaithful several times throughout their short marriage.

Jess believed that Mark was seeing a psychiatrist to try and sort out his issues and save their marriage, and the appointments were on Friday evenings, just as had been written in *SK Confessions*:

> It was a very convenient and perfectly credible cover story and I saw the merit in keeping the illusion going for the purpose of my late night freedom. So every Friday I would leave the house, and prep for a kill while my wife was convinced my shrink was working his magic. I even added the special performance of seeming lighter and more relaxed when I walked back into the house. It was only partially an act since I did in fact feel good about my evening, just not in the way Tess quite expected.

She also told police that she called him that Friday night, after 9 pm, and asked where he was, and he said he was at the gym, with a conversation that followed the script almost to the letter. She couldn't remember when Mark returned home that night. However, she had spent most of the next day with Mark and didn't notice anything particularly off about him. His mood was normal, she said, and normal for Mark was: "easy-going, kind of relaxed."

The picture that was building up about Mark Twitchell was not pretty. Jess told them the trouble in their marriage began when the two of them had a serious conversation in late September, when Mark told her he was unsure if he could feel empathy like other people. Shocked at this admission, but trying to unpack his comment, Jess had given him the example of an episode of Oprah she saw about a woman who mistakenly left her baby in the car and it died. She said as a new mother she felt a great deal of empathy for this woman. Mark responded that he understood it was sad, but it had nothing to do with him. This upset Jess, and she suggested counseling, as she did not feel comfortable being with a person who couldn't feel empathy.

Detectives also discovered that Mark had previously been married to Megan Twitchell, a US citizen, from 2001 until 2004 when she had served him with divorce papers citing "extreme and repeated mental cruelty."

In another file found on Mark Twitchell's computer, called *Profile of a Psychopath*, it appeared he had self-diagnosed, evaluating himself against the traits of a psychopath in the DSM IV Manual, considered the bible of mental disorders among psychologists. In the document, Mark detailed the extent he went to in deceiving his wife and other people. He lied about having a job and went out to great lengths to fake documents to get the mortgage, which he paid off with the money he got from investors for his films:

```
I lie to my wife and to my family on a
practically constant basis. Sometimes
I do this to protect them, to shield
them from knowing the truth about what
I really am and sometimes I do it for
my own gratification and there's no
reason to it all.
   For example I tricked a mortgage
broker and their lender into giving me
a mortgage I never could have gotten
```

otherwise. Like many psychopaths, I have trouble holding down a job because I get bored very easily, waste company time and resources and will often quit or get fired within 4 months of being hired. In my own personal case I do this because I consider working for anyone other than myself unbearable servitude . . .

I still lie to my wife to this day. Every day I get up and get dressed into business attire, feed her a line about my appointments for the day and then leave the house for the day. I set up shop in a coffee shop and work towards producing my film all day long. Then I come home, lie about how it went and move on with our free time.

However I needed that day job to get a mortgage, I needed to keep it to be approved on the basis of relia-bility and stability. . .

So I did what I had to do. I used my steadily building credit rating and ingenuity to manufacture precisely what the broker needed to close the deal. I invented a new person, named Jim Mcdougal who I passed off as the HR manager at ADT. I got a prepaid cell phone and created a false voice-mail as him. I affected my voice so that it literally sounded like an

older, more mild mannered man and it
fooled everyone. I even talked to the
lender directly as Jim confirming
details about my employment that were
totally untrue. Then I photoshopped
bank statements to hide where certain
funds came from for the down payment,
created a few fake letters of confirmation and presto, mortgage approval.

Profile of a Psychopath went into detail of the psychological torture Mark inflicted on both his wives, taking great
delight in gaslighting them, going to extraordinary lengths
to convince them that his infidelity was all in their heads. He
cheated on his wives not because he felt unfulfilled, but
because he could. When Jess caught him red-handed logged
into the Ashley Madison website, a site for married people
looking for infidelities, Mark said he'd been hired to write
an article about dating websites. He set up an elaborate plot
of fake emails and even hired an actor to play the fictional
editor on speakerphone to convince Jess he was telling the
truth. The actor had believed he was auditioning for a part.

Mark had recently begun an affair with a former girlfriend, Traci, who had also previously broken up with him
because of his constant lying when they were together. Mark
and Traci met in his first year of college, when he was single
and she had a boyfriend. He lied to her about his age and
his background and told her he had a girlfriend so she
wouldn't think he was single and pathetic. He convinced her
to date him for a while, but his lies caught up with him
when she met his parents and she learned his true age and
origins. Mark claimed to have been "absolutely devastated"
when she left.

In the fall of 2008, Mark reconnected with Traci. They started going on coffee dates and went to matinee movies when Jess thought he was at work. When they went to see a low-budget horror film called *Quarantine*, neither of them cared for it, so they spent the majority of the time kissing like teenagers in the back row.

There was a time, late in October, when Traci messaged him, and he was in such a hurry to get to her house to have sex with her, that he got pulled over for speeding, though he managed to talk the officer down to a smaller fine. After sex, Mark traced his finger around the tattoo that Traci got when she was dating him in 1997. It was a Celtic cross, about three inches in diameter, which Mark had helped design. He must have found it amusing to later incorporate the tattoo into his story about the mysterious car seller. It was a trick straight out of *The Usual Suspects*, where the story being told by the pathetic Verbal (Kevin Spacey) was all a smokescreen so the detectives interviewing him would never realize he was the master criminal Keyser Soze.

With his obsession with filmmaking, Mark would have loved to be compared to Keyser Soze. Those who spoke with him noted he was always able to bring any conversation back to whichever film he was currently working on. He was convinced of his own brilliance as a film producer and loved to drop names whenever he could. He was deluded about the quality of his films and the chances that he was going to become a Hollywood heavyweight.

Mark was also obsessed with *Dexter*, a popular book and television series in which the main character, Dexter Morgan, worked as a blood-spatter analyst with the police. Dexter also happened to be a serial killer, trained by his father to choose victims that it was morally right to kill, those who would do more harm to innocent people if they were allowed to live. He called it The Code, and Dexter had to work at maintaining a normal façade because simple acts, like smiling for photos or appearing appropriately sad at somber occasions, did not come naturally to him. In the books and TV series, Dexter Morgan went to great lengths to dispose of all evidence of his crimes, dismembering bodies in rooms covered in plastic. Dexter described his "Dark Passenger," which was both his alter-ego and the personification of his desire to kill.

Another document downloaded from Mark's computer was the script for *House of Cards*. In the short movie, which would run for less than ten minutes, a man called Roger was lured away from his wife by a woman on a dating website for cheating spouses. When he arrived at the location for their tryst, he was instead greeted by a masked man, who tortured and killed him, as punishment for his infidelity. The masked man was revealed to be a serial killer, and the film had a twist ending: after the decapitation and dismemberment of Roger, the script changed settings to a suburban house:

```
A writer leans back from staring
intensely at his laptop screen and
puts his hands behind his head taking
a deep sigh in relief that he's just
finished something solid. He closes
Microsoft Word and a website showing
the inside workings of a female
profile on a cheaters dating site is
the last thing to shut down. . .He
puts it into his carrying case and
leans over to close a duffel bag
containing gloves, a stun gun and a
```

```
black   mouthless   hockey   mask   with
yellow streaks on it.
```

The final line as the writer kissed his wife goodbye was:

```
It's true when they say the best way
to succeed is to write what you know.
```

Detectives had to ask themselves: had Mark Twitchell lured Johnny Altinger to the garage in order to film his actual murder? Was art imitating life, or was life imitating art?

The police tracked down the actors who had worked on *House of Cards*. The man who played the deranged masked murderer, Robert Barnsley, said he'd had a lot of fun on set and had enjoyed the idea of playing a serial killer. Chris Heward, the actor who had played the part of the murder victim, told the police everything he could remember about the job, including his unease at discovering the weapons that Mark used for the scene were genuine.

The detective asked how much blood was spattered on the floor and walls for the scene, and Chris confirmed that there was none. He also said he couldn't recall a barrel in the garage, nor had he seen anything resembling body parts.

Chris Heward left his interview with police with the distinct impression that, rather than a bit part in an indie film, he had somehow barely escaped playing the lead role in a snuff movie.

AN ARREST

Evidence continued to mount against Mark Twitchell. The scrapings from the metal thread of the pipe found in Mark's garage came back as containing numerous tiny fragments of skin, fat, skeletal muscle, fibrous tissue, and bone. A tooth fragment found on the floor of the garage was determined to be a human incisor. The DNA samples collected from forks, straws, juice bottles, and a drinking glass in Johnny Altinger's apartment were compared to samples obtained from Johnny's mother and brother, and then tested against evidence seized by police.

On October 31, 2008, Mark Twitchell was arrested and charged with first-degree murder. Police had received confirmation that the blood on a knife in a sheath found in his Grand AM, blood found on a duffel bag in the car, on several items in the game processing kit, as well as blood found on a pair of jeans in Mark's bedroom all matched Johnny Altinger.

Police would have preferred to have a body before charging their suspect with first-degree murder, but the amount of forensic evidence they had was overwhelming. What's more, police believed they had a 42-page written confession that they had found on Mark's computer. Everything they could verify could be precisely matched to real-life events.

Of course, Mark Twitchell would argue that *SK Confessions* was pure fiction, with certain aspects drawn from bits and pieces of his life, as so many authors do. The detectives needed to prove that deadly events outlined in the document had occurred. And if they couldn't find Johnny Altinger, maybe they could find 'Frank'.

If SK Confessions was a factual account, Johnny was not Mark Twitchell's first intended victim. That was someone the document referred to as Frank, the killer's very first target ever. The story said about luring Frank to the garage: "I roped him in with a profile I was quite proud of, featuring photos of a blonde I would like to bang myself."

Frank received the same detailed instructions that Johnny had received. The killer waited for him wearing his special mask, which he claimed served the dual purpose of hiding his identity and protecting him from blood spatter. SK Confessions said:

```
My kill room was perfectly prepped.
Plastic sheeting taped together and
around my table; a large green cloth
screwed into the drywall ceiling to
shield view of it from my guests line
of sight, and to shield me too of
course. I now stood but a few feet
away from the front door which I had
locked of course. The plan was to wait
in the shadow of my curtain until he
```

approached the door and shock him with the stun baton followed by a sleeper hold that would sap away his consciousness so that I could tape him up and set him on my table.

The last thought that crossed my mind before Frank pulled up into the driveway had nothing to do with the event itself, but rather was a mental note that I would need to remember to get a stock of paper towels for miscellaneous clean up in the future.

At the allotted time, a man entered the garage through the half-open door. The killer was waiting in his gold and black hockey mask, wearing a hoodie and brandishing a stun baton, a type of taser. Several pages of the manuscript detailed what happened next: the ensuing scuffle, the wounds the killer inflicted, how the man managed to break away, and the killer's frustration when his victim flagged down a couple who didn't seem inclined to help him but nevertheless provided him the opportunity to make it to his car and escape the clutches of the murderer.

Reading this astonishing story, the detectives soon pieced together the report that had been made by the couple in the area, with the incident relayed in *SK Confessions*. What they couldn't understand was why the victim had never come forward to make a complaint.

They knew they had to find the mysterious Frank to see if his story matched that which was in the deleted file on Mark Twitchell's computer. So far, every verifiable piece of evidence matched what was in the document. If this man's story also matched up, it was stronger evidence than ever that *SK Confessions* was, in fact, a written confession of the crimes of Mark Twitchell.

They decided to go public with the story, showcasing the black and gold hockey mask, hoping that the man would come forward.

THE ONE WHO GOT AWAY

Gilles Tetreault was looking for love when he logged onto the Plenty of Fish dating website in the summer of 2008. Newly separated at thirty-three, Gilles felt like being single was the end of the world. The breakup wasn't his choice. Using the profile name "Dr_x," he spent hours scrolling through profiles of attractive women who seemed to share his interests and hobbies. Slowly, he began to believe that he could move past his ex and find love again.

In September 2008, Gilles came across the profile of a user named "spiderwebzz." Her pictures on the dating website depicted an attractive 'girl next door' blonde in her thirties. She wrote that she was new to Edmonton and looking to meet new people. Noticing that she was online as he was checking her profile, Gilles impulsively decided to send her an instant message and was thrilled when she responded right away. She told him her real name was Sheena.

They exchanged a series of messages on the site, and Sheena's responses were friendly and forward. When she asked what Gilles was doing that weekend and he told her he had no plans, Sheena invited him to dinner and a movie in South Edmonton on October 3, 2008. When Sheena asked him to pick her up for the date, Gilles readily agreed.

Sheena told him that the only way to reach her basement apartment at the back of the house was through the door of the detached garage. She didn't provide an address but instead gave complicated instructions on how to get to the southside garage from his neighborhood. She also didn't provide her phone number, citing safety reasons. Gilles understood. There were plenty of creeps on these dating sites, and numerous stories of women being stalked.

Gilles didn't tell anyone where he was going that day and arrived a little late for the date, not having allowed himself enough time between finishing work and getting to the other side of the city. He parked right in front of the garage door, facing it. Running fifteen minutes late, and without any means to call Sheena and inform her, Gilles hurried through the partially open roll-up door and headed straight for the door at the back of the garage, which Sheena had said led to the yard and her apartment.

As he touched the doorknob, someone came up behind him, put him in a bear hug, and before he knew it, he was being struck repeatedly on the back of his head with a blunt object. Assuming he was being mugged, Gilles turned to face his attacker who was wearing a black and gold hockey mask, with the mouth cut out.

Gilles tried to escape his assailant's grasp, but instead of hitting him with the black object, the attacker was now activating it so that blue electrical charges were coming at him, and Gilles realized he was being tasered. He was surprised to discover the pain wasn't as severe as he'd anticipated, but it was irritating, so he grabbed the end of the baton to push it away. His attacker growled in frustration when he saw the stun baton wasn't effective before dropping it and pulling a gun from his pocket, demanding Gilles to get down on the ground. Knowing he couldn't compete with a firearm, Gilles obeyed. Once he laid down, the man in the mask covered his eyes with gray duct tape. Despair washed over Gilles as he realized he hadn't told anyone he was going on this date. No one knew where he was. He was surprised to discover that the cliché of your life flashing before your eyes when you're about to die was actually true.

It was when he heard jingling, like the sound of a belt buckle, that Gilles decided he had to fight back. He staggered to his feet, tore the duct tape from his eyes, and reached out and grabbed the gun barrel. Then, he experienced the best feeling he'd ever felt in his life—the gun was obviously plastic.

That gave Gilles the determination to fight for his life. Grabbing a pair of nearby black heavy-duty handcuffs, he tried to hit his assailant with them, but the man punched him in the side of the head. Gilles was still weak from the attack, but a chance presented itself when the masked man grabbed hold of the lightweight jacket Gilles had thrown on at the last minute. Gilles was able to slip out of his jacket and then roll out under the garage door, leaving his jacket behind in the clutches of the attacker. He tried to stand up and run, but his legs wouldn't cooperate, and he fell face-first on the gravel driveway. Although the stun baton hadn't been painful, it had succeeded in reducing his muscles to jelly. He dug his nails into the gravel to claw his way out, but the man in the mask reached under the door, grabbed his legs, and started dragging him back into the garage, caveman style. Gilles frantically looked around for people to scream to for help, as his fingers scrambled for holds on the ground that weren't there.

He was given one last chance when the attacker had to let go for a moment to duck under the door. Using every last bit of strength, Gilles managed to get to his feet and started to run as fast as he could, down the alley and toward a nearby walking path.

That's when he stumbled into the path of Marisa Girhiny and Trevor Hossinger and yelled at them, "There's a guy attacking me, he's mugging me, please help me!" Although the couple refused to assist him, he was able to get to his truck and drive away.

As Gilles drove home, the adrenaline wore off and everything began to hurt at once. He pulled over, retching but unable to vomit. He splashed water over his face from the bottle he kept in his truck and passed out for fifteen minutes, before going home and lying down with a towel and a pack of frozen vegetables pressed to his head.

When Gilles woke up a few hours later, he logged onto plentyoffish.com to download the messages as evidence for the police. The "spiderwebzz" profile and all the messages they'd exchanged were gone. It was as though she'd never existed. The only proof he had was the directions he had copied and pasted into a text document for printing.

Not feeling ready to face the police, Gilles called his ex-wife and told her about his ordeal in great detail. She urged him to report it, and he agreed he would. However, by the next day, he was feeling ashamed and embarrassed. Dating websites were still somewhat taboo in 2008, not yet having gained widespread social acceptance. It was humiliating to have been tricked into believing he was meeting an attractive woman who he genuinely thought liked him as much as he liked her. He felt like a loser.

As the pain subsided over the next couple of days, he began to tell himself that perhaps the whole thing hadn't been as severe as he initially thought. It was probably just a mugging that hadn't gone according to plan. He couldn't hide the cuts and bruises, so he was forced to tell his friends and coworkers about the encounter. All of them urged him to go to the police, but Gilles just wanted to put the whole incident behind him.

~

ON NOVEMBER 2, 2008, Gilles was awakened by a ringing phone and notifications of several missed calls from his friend Andrew. Andrew urged him to get online and check out an article in the *Edmonton Journal*, a local newspaper that had been reporting on the disappearance of Johnny Altinger from the time he'd been reported missing. Andrew thought that the sparse details in the article sounded like what had happened to Gilles. The article said that a man had been arrested for the murder of Johnny Altinger and that police were searching for a first victim, whom they believed had been lured to the garage by a fake female dating profile.

As he read the article, Gilles Tetreault's blood ran cold. The story of Johnny Altinger was more than eerily familiar to him, and he would never forget that hockey mask. As he later wrote in his memoir, *The One Who Got Away*, "I realized that I should have been the one who was killed and my body should have been hacked up into pieces... Worse, I started to think that if only I had gone to the police, John Brian Altinger might be alive and well right now. If I had just gone like I said I would, nobody would have been killed and dismembered. Guilt overwhelmed me."

On November 3, Gilles presented himself to the Edmonton Police station, where he was interrogated and quizzed for several hours about the ordeal he had gone through the previous month. His story matched almost word-for-word the attack on "Frank" described in *SK Confessions*.

MARK'S SECRET LIFE

New evidence continued to surface after Mark Twitchell's arrest. On November 5, a woman named Renee Waring, from Cleveland, Ohio, sent the Edmonton Police chat logs she had saved from a social media profile that sported a profile picture of the serial killer, Dexter Morgan. She was a huge fan of the show and had no idea who was behind the Facebook profile—she harbored hopes that it might actually belong to the actor who played Dexter. The two engaged in banter back and forth until finally the Dexter profile admitted to being an indie film producer named Mark and shared a link to his production company website.

Their conversations carried on through private messages, and the discussions increasingly took a dark turn. When Renee told Mark that she fantasized about dismembering her ex-husband's new wife and creating patterns in the woman's blood, he responded with detailed advice and instructions on how to do it and get away with it. Mark suggested it would be better to construct a "kill room," just like Dexter's, lined with plastic, where she could lure the new wife and incapacitate her with a stun baton.

He advised that it would be wise to wrap the body from head to toe in duct tape and put the pieces in numerous large, extra-strength trash bags. He proposed she would want to pulverize the jawbone and remove the teeth, as well as the fingertips, to avoid identification and, ideally, incinerate the entire body, though that might take some time.

In a new Facebook message, sent on October 5, Mark suggested to Renee that a stun baton might prove ineffective. This message was sent two days after he'd had that exact issue with his failed attempt on Gilles Tetreault. He suggested a sturdy copper pipe, taped at one end, would work better. This was eerily similar to the one police had removed from the garage, which was stained with Johnny Altinger's blood and brain matter.

Breaking up the body by hand would be difficult, Mark wrote, but he assured her: "A hunter's game processing kit comes with everything you'd need to cut the body into manageable pieces."

Their correspondence continued until she received a message from him on October 10 at 3:22 p.m. It read: "Sorry this is so short, but I'm juggling six things right now and it's time to pare down to five." That was the day Johnny Altinger disappeared.

Four days later, she received another message from Mark on Facebook. He wrote: "This weekend, I made the rounds to two family Thanksgiving events and I've also had something else keeping me busy. But I'm really hesitant about telling anyone because of the implications. Suffice it to say, I crossed the line on Friday, and I liked it."

Friday was the day Johnny Altinger had been murdered.

She next heard from him on October 27, this time via

email, when he told her his marriage was ending and there was a missing person investigation, possibly a homicide, related to the garage he used. He assured her that he was confident they wouldn't find anything and also asked her not to inquire about the details. Mark wrote: "Of course, all my recent ventures into darker fiction don't look good in all of this."

WHAT HAPPENED TO JOHNNY

Police had no doubt that, even without a body, they knew exactly what had happened to Johnny Altinger. It was described with relish over dozens of pages in the aspiring serial killer's memoir.

The man, referred to as "Jim" in *SK Confessions*—but who police were convinced was Johnny—entered hopefully through the partially open garage door, just as "Jen" had instructed. When he saw the same man as before there instead of the blonde and enticing Jen, Johnny said cheerfully, "I guess I'm just a glutton for punishment."

Mark replied, "You have no idea." Then, according to the story:

```
The room filled with the echo of the
pipe crashing into the back of his
skull as I could feel my predator self
take over. That one single motion was
the end all be all. I had committed
now and there was no going back.
```

SK Confessions went into gleeful, gory detail of the ensuing hours. It described Johnny's desperate attempts to escape, his adrenaline fueling his actions, even as the killer struck him over and over again with the pipe.

```
He began screaming at the top of his
lungs. "Police! Police! Police!" and I
just about shat my pants. My fury
doubled and I blasted him so hard
blood  spattered  everywhere,  but
primarily on me. He hit the floor but
was still conscious.
```

Johnny frantically tried to bribe the killer, offering money and a promise not to go to the police—actions that earned him a sneer and another beating. Mark was surprised by just how long it was taking to knock Johnny out. Finally, he wrote:

```
I pulled my hunting knife from its
sheath and watching the shock on his
face as he saw the blade, I thrust it
into his gut. His reaction was pure
Hollywood. The lurch forward with the
grunt was dead-on TV movie of the
week.
```

Johnny moaned and the killer plunged the knife deep into his neck. As he watched Johnny die, Mark reflected on the fact that no matter how meticulously everything is planned, nothing ever goes exactly as it should. He had intended to trick Johnny into giving up his debit PIN code by pretending he would call an ambulance, but had forgotten in the heat of the moment. There was blood every-where, and he'd forgotten to fully close the garage door.

> I let him bleed out right there on the floor, away from the plastic sheeting specifically put up to avoid that sort of thing. But hey I had bigger problems. I had no real idea if a jogger, a dog walker, an unconvinced neighbor or some other random individual had actually called the cops, just as a precaution.
>
> I was standing there covered in blood. It was all over my face, my hoody, my coat and my jeans. I was holding the murder weapon in my hand standing over what would be in moments, a corpse, and not nearly enough time to make it go away.

Once Mark confirmed Johnny was dead, he hoisted Johnny onto the custom-made table ("I should really stick to smaller guys from now on"), removed his keys and wallet, which he set aside, then stripped off all his clothes, leaving his underwear and shoes and socks on ("I don't need to see my victim's dead junk hanging out while I'm trying to work"). He then pulled out his brand new game processing kit and examined each of the knives and tools in turn, determining what each one was for and how best they could be used for the task at hand.

The killer poked and prodded the joints to find the path of least resistance and began cutting off the legs at the knees. He was surprised to discover how easily the knife cut through flesh, even the tendons and ligaments. Tossing the severed leg into the trash, he moved up to the thigh and then the arms, before finally decapitating his victim. As he bagged up the limbs and head, eventually just the torso remained on the table. He wrote:

```
I  noticed  that  it  wasn't  nearly  as
horrendous  as  the  media  made  it  look
on  TV  or  in  movies.  Dismembering  a
human  body  was  a  relatively  unexciting
event.  But  I  had  my  ways  of  making  it
more  fun.  I  sang  to  myself  as  I
worked,  talked  to  myself,  reflected  on
the  new  tools  I  would  get  to  make  the
next  one  easier.
```

Once he had dismembered Johnny, placing him into several bags, he started the arduous task of cleaning the garage and himself, pausing to take a call from Jess, to whom he calmly said he was at the gym. He loaded all the pieces of Johnny into Johnny's Mazda, which he moved into the garage, then went home to his wife and little girl.

That weekend, Mark broke into Johnny's home and stole his laptop so he could update Johnny's social media status and respond to any inquiring friends via email. Next, he had to figure out how to dispose of the body. The document revealed:

```
Incineration.  I  had  looked  into
buying  an  actual  batch  incinerator.
Something  with  the  pressure  and  heat
needed  to  get  the  job  done.  The
problem  with  those  are  they  cost
```

```
upwards of $5,000 to acquire and I
wouldn't be in a position to make
that purchase for another month or
two. I had a jerrycan of gasoline in
my trunk and a steel drum though.
Close enough.
```

On Monday morning, he loaded the entire drum—limbs, torso, and all—into the back seat of Johnny's car and took it all to his parents' house. He hadn't lied to the police when he said he couldn't drive a manual transmission, but "necessity is the mother of invention," he wrote. He placed it squarely into the center of the yard. He doused the bag of torso pieces in gasoline, dropped it into the barrel, lit a match, and tossed it in. The instant whoosh of flames consuming flammable liquid erupted from the top, and the burn began.

As the body cooked in the fire, the author revealed he had no sense of smell, so he couldn't determine how bad the thick black smoke billowing out might smell to any neighbors. Mark quickly realized that burning the body wasn't going to work. He hurriedly doused it when he heard approaching sirens, worried that the neighbors had called the fire department on him.

He wrote about being so excited by the weekend's activities that he was sexually aroused and arranged to meet with his former girlfriend, Traci (named Laci in the document). He was in such a rush to get to her house that he was pulled over by the police. He chuckled to himself that they had no way of knowing they were talking to a psychopath who had just killed and dismembered a man.

That night he had the best sex he'd ever had.

The next day, he returned to the problem of disposing of

Johnny Altinger's body. He decided he needed to cut it into much smaller pieces:

> I took out one of the arms. It was stiff and cold, rigor mortis having set in by now. It was also quite brisk outside today since it was fall heading into winter. I was grateful for the temperature though since my outfit was warm and I would be doing quite a bit of physical activity today.
>
> I chose the butcher knife to start out with and simply shaved the meat from the bone in a downward motion. I didn't bother getting every single shred since I knew that once dumped in the river, it would rot off in a timely fashion anyway. When it was cleared, each slab looked like a cutlet sitting on the table.
>
> I put each chunk on the cutting board and used the fillet knife to slice them into even smaller pieces. When I was satisfied with my medallion sized portions, I tossed them into the garbage bag. Very little mess was made at first.
>
> I repeated the process with the legs, thighs and upper arms. Routinely shaving the meat off them, placing the bones in a pile and filleting the meat into small pieces before tossing them

into a bag. When the bag got somewhat
heavy to lift easily, I closed it off
in the same fashion as the originals
and got a new one.

Once in a while I would take a
break, check my email, answer a few
phone calls, check the status of my
eBay page and have a bag of chips. I
got a message from Laci on Facebook
commenting on how hot the night was
and how she was looking forward to the
next time. I fantasized about the
night before and how Laci and been a
total porn star in the sack. I was
incredibly lucky. When I realised two
hours had passed I decided to do the
head next. I sliced the face off in
several different pieces, cut the ears
and lips up so the again, they
couldn't be visually identified. This
way if someone did see it floating in
a river, they would think nothing of
it anyway.

Once the flesh was removed, I used
the pipe to knock out the teeth, elim-
inating dental records as a form of
ID. I broke the jaw after that and
used the scissors to cut the ligaments, ripping the jaw clean from the
head in it's multiple pieces held
together only by the tissue at this
point. I used the knife to destroy the
eyes as well and then rammed the pipe

into the side of the skull to bust it open. At this point it was fuelled only by curiosity to see the human brain live and in person since I had never seen it before.

Removing the skin and flesh in the back was easy. These were the chunks I tried to burn the first time around so the skin was charred in some places making it more stiff in some places and easy to cut. I hacked off the ass cheeks and marvelled at how fatty they were for such a slim person. I immediately thought of the movie Alive and how all the rugby team must have feasted on this part of the human body while trapped in the Andes. But the freezer burn from the bodies being in the snow and frozen solid might have ruined the experience. Well that and the trauma of realising you're eating a dead person but that never entered by thinking at all. Meat is meat after all. It tastes like beef or chicken.

Once that was processed, I moved on to my final piece, the upper torso. I started with shaving the outside, taking all off the skin, muscle and fat in single pieces, like I was carving a turkey. In fact, once every-thing else had been removed, I was surprised at how closely the chest

```
cavity resembles the overall shape of
a turkey.
     This was the messy portion. All of
the blood that hadn't come out was
inside this piece, trapped in the
lungs, still close to the heart. It
dumped out onto the table, not quite
enough to overflow to the floor or
anything but messy nonetheless. I used
a knife to cut all the tissue around
the edge of the rib cage in order to
free any remaining organs. The lungs,
the heart and the liver all came out.
I cut those up too before trashing
them.
     It reminded me of emptying a
pumpkin for Halloween.
```

Mark finally finished the job, exhausted, but with all of Johnny's pieces neatly packed away into plastic bags. He was too tired to venture out into the night to dispose of the body and decided to return early the next day, when he would find a place to deposit the bags in the river.

The document that had been recovered from Mark Twitchell's laptop ended abruptly as he drove around in search of the ideal spot to enter the water. However, a computer forensic analyst with the Edmonton Police found a file on a desktop computer at Mark Twitchell's parents' home that seemed to be a continuation of the writings. The new text began:

```
The sewer. Of course, how obvious. No
one ever goes down there. The body
```

would   rot   away   completely   before
anyone   ever   discovered   the   bones   and
by   then   it   would   be   way   too   late   to
identify   the   person.

The detectives were confident they were finally going to
find the remains of Johnny Altinger.

SEARCHING FOR JOHNNY

The author of *SK Confessions* had written that, after failing to properly cremate the body, he bagged up the limbs, torso, and head again and stuffed them into nearby sewers. As the police had established that Mark had attempted to burn the body in a barrel at his parents' place (thanks to the memoir explicitly stating that, and the barrel-sized burn mark on their backyard), on November 5, 2008, police and city workers combed the area around their home, inspecting every sewer they could find. They painstakingly searched every street and alley, working outwards from the Twitchell family home. Every grate was removed, and sewer workers poked their heads, and sometimes their entire bodies, into the stinking pipes, looking for any signs of Johnny.

A video posted by *48 Hours* shows detectives driving Mark around on the search, trying to convince him that helping them locate the body would be looked upon favorably in his sentencing. Otherwise, he was looking at a minimum of twenty-five years with no chance of parole. Mark sat in the back of the unmarked car looking bored, until one of the detectives snapped, "Hey Mark, are we wasting our time here, or are you going to tell us where the body is?" Mark just blinked silently.

"You're the guy who wanted to be a serial killer but got caught on his first try," the detective taunted.

Their taunts were unsuccessful in getting anything out of Mark, and they found nothing. After an exhaustive search, they gave up. Perhaps some parts of *SK Confessions* were fiction after all. The police had enough evidence that a murder had taken place, even if they didn't have Johnny Altinger's body. They set about the task of ensuring that this evidence was enough to convict Mark Twitchell of first-degree murder.

As is the case with capital murder charges, things moved slowly. Mark Twitchell was held in jail as he awaited his trial, feverishly drawing pictures and writing stories to pass the time.

~

THE INVESTIGATORS in the case had all but given up on recovering a body, and Johnny's family had resigned themselves to never being able to give him a proper burial. Then, shortly after 6 p.m. on June 3, 2010, homicide detectives were called to meet Mark Twitchell and his attorney at the Remand Center. It was a year and a half after Johnny Altinger's disappearance, and Mark was yet to go to trial. After being reminded of his rights and agreeing he understood them, Mark passed the detectives a piece of paper that had been folded in half. It was a Google map depicting an area of north Edmonton. Written on the map were the words "Location of John Altinger's remains".

The map directed the officers to an alley where two

manhole covers sat in close proximity to a telephone pole. The detectives followed the directions on the map and found the sewer, as it was described on the folded piece of paper. When they peered through the grate, what appeared to be two pieces of human remains lay in the darkness. It was just one block away from where police had stopped their sweep of the sewers in November 2008.

Office investigator Dennis Caulfield suited up in coveralls and boots and descended into the sewer. He recovered bones from an upper and lower torso, along with some decomposed soft tissue. Notably absent were any identifiable human organs.

The medical examiners recovered teeth from the sediment around the torso. Less than half of the bones of a human body were recovered, but they all seemed to be from one person, and that person was Johnny Altinger.

Johnny's family could finally give him the burial he deserved.

THE DEXTER TRIAL

The long-anticipated trial began on March 16, 2011, following an intense media blackout. Once the blackout was lifted, they reported with relish, as there had never been a trial like this before.

The prosecution laid out its case from all the evidence meticulously gathered by Edmonton law enforcement. One hundred twelve police officers were involved in the investigation, including thirteen homicide detectives, seven forensics officers, and eighty-one patrol officers.

As the witnesses came to the stand one by one, the prosecutors skillfully laid out their case that Mark Twitchell had lured strangers to his "kill room," where he planned to attack them, replicating elements and methods used by fictional serial killer Dexter Morgan. He had done so with premeditation and intent to kill.

The document titled *Profile of a Psychopath*, in which Mark provided a detailed self-analysis of personality and behavior that matched the traits of a psychopath in the DSM IV manual of mental disorders, was not allowed into evidence. The judge ruled that the document was too inflammatory to be read to jurors, and would compromise the trial.

However, *SK Confessions* was an integral part of the prosecution's case. Lead investigator Mark Anstey went through the document, line by line, and identified three hundred one passages that were deemed to be provable real-life occurrences. Detectives were called to the stand to prove or disprove each one of these selected passages by matching them to real-life events they knew to be true.

Detectives involved in the case, forensic specialists, both of Mark's former wives, his girlfriend, and the woman he corresponded with as "Dexter" all provided testimony. Friends of both Mark and Johnny were also called to the stand to have their recollections of events presented to the court. The testimony of Gilles Tetreault and the couple, Marisa Girhiny and Trevor Hossinger, never wavered, and they matched the details in the confessions document precisely.

After their testimony, Marisa and Trevor were desperate to meet Gilles and apologize to him for not assisting him in his time of need. Gilles met the couple and graciously forgave them. He understood carrying a burden of guilt, as he carried his own from not coming forward at the time of his assault. If he had gone to the police, Johnny Altinger might still be alive.

The prosecution drew their case to a close with an overwhelming amount of evidence that Mark Twitchell had not only killed Johnny Altinger, but had written what amounted to a forty-five-page confession about it. Then it was the defense's turn.

Aside from a couple of witnesses who were questioned briefly, the defense's key witness was Mark Twitchell himself. He had given up his right to remain silent because he wanted to testify. It was his chance to turn on the theatrics, to give the performance of his life, and the whole country was watching.

To gasps in the courtroom, Mark admitted that he had, in fact, killed Johnny Altinger. However, he had done so in self-defense.

Mark's testimony was long and involved. Mostly his answers were to the point, almost terse, except when he was talking about his film projects. Then he would get animated and excited, occasionally smiling, and willing to talk at length. He had the audience he had always craved.

He admitted to writing the script for *House of Cards*, to renting the garage and purchasing the barrel and various knives and other items, which he said were to be used as props in the film. The heavy pipe he bought as a model to make a rubber copy. The game processing kit, which had no role in the film, was for a future episode, Mark having decided that *House of Cards* was going to become an ambitious, interactive project that blurred what was real and what was not, which he called 'Multi-Angle Psychosis Layering Entertainment'. The concept had the catchy acronym: MAPLE.

He wanted to build on the buzz created by concepts like the *Blair Witch Project*, which was marketed as genuine found footage from a video camera rather than a professionally produced film. Mark's concept was to release a feature film about a serial killer who occasionally breaks the fourth wall, addressing the audience. The film would depict a serial killer living a seemingly normal life, which would plant an element of doubt in the audience's mind: the idea that anyone among them could be a sociopath.

After the film, he would release a novel, told from the perspective of the film's producer. The idea was to sow additional seeds of doubt about whether the film depicted real events, leading the audience "down the rabbit hole," trying to figure out if the events truly happened. He said he hoped it would function somewhat like *The Matrix*, where some people were left wondering if they were actually in the computer-generated world depicted in that film as they left the theater. He wanted to make the audience question whether his film was fact or fiction, and whether there truly was a serial killer in a gold and black hockey mask at large, luring unsuspecting men on dating sites.

The third step would be to harness social media, creating posts and fake news from people who claimed to be involved, who might have seen the room from the movie and book in real life, or who had almost been a victim of the killer themselves. It would be ideal if some of those accounts were from before the film came out, adding to their authenticity.

The messages Mark exchanged with Renee Waring on Facebook using the Dexter Morgan profile were, he said, part of his research into the mindset of psychopaths, and what it would feel like to think like one. But when he wrote: "Suffice it to say I crossed the line on Friday, and I liked it," what he referred to was the make-out session with Traci in the movie theater. He claimed it had nothing to do with killing Johnny.

He began writing the novel, naming it *SK Confessions* as a tribute to Stephen King, which is what he said the "SK" stood for. In it, he based many character traits on his real life but altered details to fit the narrative of the MAPLE project. To make his plan work, he needed to start the internet buzz first, with events that could be verified to have occurred before the film and book release. A component of this was luring people to the garage under the pretense of being a woman interested in sex with them. Then he would reveal the true reason for their meeting, and the two of them could work out a plan to create the online stories.

Using a photo of a blonde woman he had stolen from another plentyoffish.com profile in another state, he began the search for a target who fit the profile required for his MAPLE project. Gilles Tretreault seemed perfect, so they set up a time for him to come to the garage for what Gilles believed would be dinner and a movie.

Mark agreed that the inside of the garage was designed to resemble a kill room because he wanted to create the right effect. The plan was that he would explain the concept when Gilles arrived. He would ask Gilles to go about his life, and when the film and book were released, Gilles would go online and support the concept by talking about the event actually happening. But then, at the last minute, he decided to switch it up by actually pretending to scare Gilles, convincing him that he was being attacked. He said he put on the mask and used the stun baton, which he knew wouldn't truly harm his victim. The plan was always to let him go, so that when the book and movie came out, he would be genuine and convincing when he told people about his experience. Mark admitted on the stand, "I actually didn't have a lot of time to think it through."

Mark said he kept the mask, the hoodie, the baton, and the handcuffs because he figured at that point it would be best to come clean if Gilles did report what had happened.

The following week he was using the name "Jen" and photographs of a redhead to communicate with Johnny Altinger. The interaction between them went back and forth over a couple of days before they set a time and day to meet at the garage, this time for a sexual encounter.

Mark said he arrived at the garage around 6 p.m. that

night and set up the laptop he was using to communicate with Johnny prior to his arrival at the garage. He had more lights in the garage than he had when Gilles arrived the previous week, and he decided to leave the mask out of it.

When Johnny arrived earlier than expected, Mark told him he was the person working in the garage that Jen had told him to expect. He showed him around and threw up the smoke screen that Jen wasn't there yet. As he showed him different props, he said Johnny seemed to humor him and then politely excused himself. When Johnny returned, Mark was pretending to wrap up a phone call with the imaginary Jen and told Johnny she was stuck in traffic. He told Johnny she wouldn't be able to make it to the garage for at least 30 minutes.

Johnny decided not to stay, and Mark went back on the computer, wondering if Johnny was on the phone, describing what had happened, already building a buzz. He wondered whether he should reveal to Johnny over email or in person that he'd been lured under false pretenses. He ultimately decided to invite Altinger back to the garage for a third time. He emailed Altinger again, still posing as Jen.

When Johnny came back to the garage for a third time, Mark testified that he revealed that there was no Jen and tried to explain his "psychosis layering" idea. Johnny was none too happy at having been duped, and the two got into an argument. Mark claimed that as he turned his back on him, the next thing he remembered was an impact in his lower back as Johnny kicked him.

He said Johnny had grabbed a pipe and swung it. Mark dodged the first couple of swings, but the third blow came down on his elbow. He managed to grab the pipe and then swung at Johnny, the pipe catching him on the top of the head.

In the ensuing struggle, Mark continued to hit him, just trying to get him to stop, but Johnny kept at him. Eventually, frightened, Mark grabbed a knife, hoping that would cause Johnny to back off, but instead, Johnny came rushing at him with the pipe. That's when Mark stabbed him. He told the court, "It was just the sickest feeling ever. I just started to feel this wet sensation around the hand still holding the handle, and I let go, instinctively. And then I saw it sticking out of him." As he realized Johnny was not going to live, he said, "It's one of those moments when I'm just stuck there and can't decide what to do. I'm just frozen by inaction. There's a war going on between screaming out in my head: Call 911! But at the same time: How bad does this look? Take a look around. Look at what this place looks like."

Mark said he panicked and decided to use his film set: "to do things it had never been designed to do." From that part on, he agreed that the dismemberment, attempted burning of the body, the eventual hiding of pieces of Johnny's body in the sewer, and the visit to Johnny's apartment to send out emails to his friends and update his social media, went pretty much as he had described in *SK Confessions*. However, the feelings he described in the manuscript when cutting up the body the second time were exactly the opposite of the truth, he said. He felt weaker, not stronger, as though he was carrying a serious burden that he would never be able to share.

Mark said he was apprehensive and nervous when the detectives were questioning him, trying to buy some time. He thought if he could get funding for one of his movies, he would be able to give the money to his family to take care of them while he was in prison.

Mark's attorney summed up, saying that Johnny's death had been accidental and that *SK Confessions* was a work of fiction, or at best a fictionalized version of certain real events. He said, "This was not supposed to be a document about accidental death. This was not supposed to be a document about a need to defend oneself from a fight. This was supposed to be a story about the character's progression into becoming a serial killer. It was written intending to fit within a certain genre. It was intended to jar the reader, and chill the reader, and shock the reader. The reason he wrote it up as a murder: that was the whole point of the storyline he was working on."

On cross-examination, the Crown prosecutor pointed out the obvious. The killer in *SK Confessions* said all of the weapons in the garage could be explained away as props, just as Mark was doing right there on the stand. Aside from a couple of minor inconsistencies, nearly every verifiable sentence in that document could be matched to a real-life event. It seemed incredibly coincidental that the only time events varied from the story was when Mark and Johnny were alone in that garage.

The prosecutor pointed out that Mark Twitchell's entire life was built on fantasy and lies, and that his testimony should be taken with a grain of salt. He lied to his wife, to his girlfriend, to his friends, and the police. He lied about having a job. He lied when he lured Johnny and Gilles to his garage.

The jury heard about Mark's ability to come up with quick lies, like the one he told Jess about the gym, while Johnny was still lying on the table, not even having had the chance to go cold. They also heard of the elaborate lengths he went to in maintaining his lies, like when he hired an actor to play his editor to deceive his wife and faked an entire HR Department to obtain a mortgage.

The prosecutor said that Mark's most elaborate lie of all

was the Multi-Angle Psychosis Layering Entertainment. The notion that everything can be explained by his new and revolutionary idea MAPLE, a plan to blend fiction with fact by recruiting strangers to help him create an online urban legend was "as ridiculous as the story about the forty-dollar Mazda."

The jury took just a few short hours to deliberate. At 5:45 pm on April 12, 2011, Mark Twitchell was found guilty of first-degree murder.

He showed no reaction as the verdict was read. Johnny's mother, Elfriede, began to cry. She said in her victim-impact statement that she did not wish the death penalty on Twitchell, but that she wanted him to reflect on what he'd done. In his statement, Gary Altinger wrote, "I know my baby brother is never coming back. For justice to prevail, it would only be right that Mark Twitchell never see the light of day again."

Mark Twitchell was sentenced to life in prison with the chance to apply for parole in twenty-five years.

LIVING WITHOUT JOHNNY

After Mark's testimony, Johnny Altinger's brother, Gary, and mother, Elfriede, faced the media. Gary told them: "Over the last several weeks, and of course over the last couple years, our family has been exposed to such grief that no human being should ever feel."

Gary described his brother as a selfless man: "He was always helping everybody. He was gentle. It's been the worst. Nothing else can be said."

Johnny's mother Elfriede said there will never be closure, but "we will move on to the next step I think, start to heal, if that's possible."

In SK Confessions, Mark had written about the type of person he would target for murder. As an avid Dexter fan, he wanted to emulate the fictional serial killer, who only kills bad people. Mark wrote:

```
At first I considered married men
looking to cheat on their wives. In
one way I'd be taking out the trash,
doling out justice to those who on
```

some level, deserved what they got. But the logic of the situation denies this possibility. After all people who are expected home at a certain hour tend to get reported as missing and there's other factors that would lead to an investigation I didn't want. No, I had to choose people whose entire lives I could infiltrate and eliminate evidence of my existence from on all levels.

I finally settled on middle-aged single men who lived alone. My reasons were numerous. For one thing, they would be easy to lead by their dicks, easy to manipulate, easy to seduce under my fake female disguises. They were also the most likely targets to have the most expendable money in their bank accounts. A tidbit I would use to my advantage later on. Finally, by living alone, once they were out of the picture I could easily enter their living spaces undetected with no forced entry and remove all sorts of valuable items from the premises.

He made up many online personas, some seeking serious dating and others casual flings, to lure his prey. As it happened, Johnny Altinger responded to two personas - one looking for a relationship and the other, "Jen," who was looking for fun times. Mark and Johnny chatted through both usernames, until Mark was satisfied he had found a perfect victim. He wrote:

```
Amongst the smart assed punks and the
creepy old fellas who frankly, would
be more suspicious of me if I gave
them the time of day than not based on
their appearances, was my target. A
six footish seemingly nice man who
appeared clean cut, not overly good
looking but not an ogre either and
most importantly, fit for the profile.
```

Unluckily for Mark, Johnny did not fit his profile in one significant respect: he had friends who cared about him and who would immediately worry the moment he didn't turn up for a planned occasion. He was also the sort of guy who actually alerted his friends as to where he was going and the kind of friend who would not let down a buddy he had promised to give a riding lesson to. He was the sort of man who attracted friends who loved him enough to take swift action when he went missing.

Detective Mark Antsey believed that Johnny saved lives by talking to his friends about his concerns with the date and emailing them the directions to the garage. Taking the precaution of letting somebody know where he was meant detectives had an immediate and solid lead of where to look. Had Johnny been like most men, Mark Twitchell would have had significantly more time to clean up after himself and there would have been no reason to suspect him of any foul play. He might have remained under the radar of police long enough to lure more victims, and it was clear that he had aspirations to become a serial killer.

Detective Antsey told Johnny's mother Elfriede: "Your son, in a roundabout way, was a hero. He definitely saved a lot of grief for other families."

Mark Twitchell tried to appeal his conviction on the grounds that the extensive media coverage ruined any opportunity for a fair trial. In his notice of appeal he wrote: "The media attention surrounding my case was so extensive, so blatant and so overtly sensationalized that it is unreasonable to expect any unsequestered jury to have remained uninfluenced by it, regardless of judge's instructions in the charge." He also wrote three pages of points that he believed had not been adequately addressed in his trial, including: "Significant differences in the philosophical worldview and individual search for meaning between myself and the [*SK Confessions*] narrator were not discussed."

This appeal was abandoned in 2012.

He fancied himself as what Vronsky termed "the postmodern serial killer" - handsome, suave and of extremely high IQ, destined to be immortalized in Netflix specials, like Ted Bundy or Ed Kemper.

From the time his incarceration began, Mark spent his time producing artwork and in 2011, he put up celebrity pencil sketches to sell on the Internet. In May 2013, it was reported that Mark had purchased a television for his prison cell. He said that he had caught up on every Dexter episode that he missed since he was arrested.

Mark Twitchell is one of hundreds of prisoners who have a profile on Canadian Inmates Connect Ltd., a Toronto-based site that helps prisoners find pen pals on the outside. His profile picture is a flattering pencil sketch of himself. He writes: "My creative engine never slows, so I produce artwork constantly and craft novels or screenplays to manifest my relentless imagination... I'm looking for an interesting, intelligent, open-minded, delightfully imperfect woman to relate to and share amusing observations with... as well as potentially a long weekend every few months if it gets there naturally." His expected release date noted on the profile is 2027.

In her victim impact statement, Johnny's mother, Elfriede, had written that the telephone company had not yet reassigned his number, so she constantly rang it just to hear his voice. She said: "He was a pure joy as a child. It was an amazing journey watching him grow in every way and make his way through life. Though he was not blessed with the best looks, he grew into a gentle, quiet, affectionate and trusting individual. He was a comfort and a pleasure to have at home, being very helpful. I missed him when he decided to move back to Edmonton with two friends to pursue job opportunities. His life had ups and downs like everyone's but he thrived in a job he liked, had old and new friends, bought a townhouse, flipped it, and bought another apartment. There are no words to describe the pain and feelings of horror one goes through. I can't imagine the fear, desperation and pain Johnny must have endured. As a mother, I feel I can't think about it without going over the edge. There is no joy in life. It has been ripped away from me. I fear this nightmare and my grief will continue until my dying day.

"People have asked me if I wish there was still the death penalty and I must answer no. My wish is for the perpetrator of this unforgivable and horrific act to reflect on his actions and die a slow death every day of his life."

AFTERWORD

This book is by no means an exhaustive list of serial killers who have incorporated the internet into their crimes, and there may be many more.

According to the FBI there are anywhere between twenty-five and fifty serial killers at large at any one time in the United States alone.

Most of them probably use the internet in some shape or form.

Keep going for more books in the Dark Webs True Crime series

ALSO BY EILEEN ORMSBY

A Manual for Murder: FREE AND EXCLUSIVE

Murder on the Dark Web: true stories from the dark side of the internet

Stalkers: true tales of deadly obsessions

Little Girls Lost: true tales of heinous crimes

Mishap or Murder? True tales of mysterious deaths and disappearances

The Darkest Web

Silk Road

Keep going for sneak peeks of these books and to find out how to get your FREE TRUE CRIME BOOK

A MANUAL FOR MURDER

THE TRUE STORY OF HOW A BOOK LED TO A TRIPLE HOMICIDE

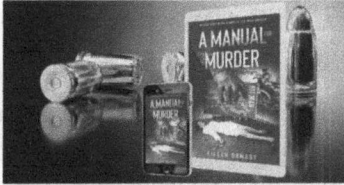

When officers attend a triple homicide in a well-to-do neighborhood in Maryland, it looks like a robbery gone wrong. But why did the intruder kill a profoundly disabled boy who had no way of identifying him?

When the FBI is called in, their investigations take them from the glamorous world of Hollywood music royalty to the seediest districts of Detroit. It looks like the killer might have been too smart for them, until they find a book in a suspect's apartment, which may be the key to unraveling it all.

GET THIS EXCLUSIVE EBOOK AT EILEENORMSBY.COM

This book is not for sale and is only available to those who sign up for my newsletter. But don't worry: I won't spam you or pass your information on to anyone else. You can unsubscribe any time you like, even right after you download your free book! I don't mind, though I do hope you will stick around for updates to the cases I write about and to be first to know about any new books

THE DARKEST WEB

The Darkest Web

Dark...

A kingpin willing to murder to protect his dark web drug empire. A corrupt government official determined to avoid exposure. The death of a dark web drugs czar in mysterious circumstances in a Bangkok jail cell, just as the author arrives there.

Who is Variety Jones and why have darknet markets ballooned tenfold since authorities shut down the original dark web drugs bazaar, Silk Road? Who are the kingpins willing to sell poisons and weapons, identities and bank accounts, malware and life-ruining services online to anyone with a wallet full of Bitcoin?

Darker...

A death in Minnesota leads detectives into the world of dark web murder-for-hire where hundreds of thousands of dollars in Bitcoin is paid to arrange killings, beatings and rapes. Meanwhile, the owner of the most successful hitman website in history is threatening the journalists who investigate his business with a visit from his operatives - and the author is at the top of his list.

Darkest...

People with the most depraved perversions gather to share their obscene materials in an almost inaccessible corner of the dark web. A video circulates and the pursuit of the monsters responsible for 'Daisy's Destruction' lead detectives into the unimaginable horror of the world of hurtcore.

There's the world wide web - the internet we all know that connects us via news, email, forums, shopping and social media. Then there's the dark web - the parallel internet accessed by only a select few. Usually, those it connects wish to remain anonymous and for good reason.

Eileen Ormsby has spent the past five years exploring every corner of the Dark Web. She has shopped on darknet markets, contributed to forums, waited in red rooms and been threatened by hitmen on murder-for-hire sites. On occasions, her dark web activities have poured out into the real world and she has attended trials, met with criminals and the law enforcement who tracked them down, interviewed dark web identities and visited them in prison.

This book will take you into the murkiest depths of the web's dark underbelly: a place of hitmen for hire, red rooms, hurtcore sites and markets that will sell anything a person is willing to pay for - including another person. The Darkest Web.

Published by Allen & Unwin

HEAD TO EILEENORMSBY.COM FOR BUYING OPTIONS

MURDER ON THE DARK WEB

TRUE STORIES FROM THE DARK SIDE OF THE INTERNET

A look into the dark side of the internet's secret underbelly

A Minnesota dog trainer is found dead of an apparent suicide after detectives find her details on a dark web murder-for-hire site. But who paid $13,000 in Bitcoin to kill this devout Christian and beloved wife and mother?

An Instagram glamour model is drugged, kidnapped and listed for sale on a dark web human trafficking site. A secret society called Black Death demands a ransom for her safe return, or else she will be sold to sadistic millionaires to use before feeding to the tigers.

The dark web is the internet's evil twin, where anything can be bought and sold. Drugs, weapons, and hackers-for-hire are available at the touch of a button.

Most who visit merely look around, happy to simply satisfy their curiosity before leaving, never to return. But some are sucked into the criminal underworld and find themselves doing things they would never have contemplated in the real world—ordering a hit on a love rival or bidding on an auction for a sex slave—like the people in this book.

These are extraordinary true tales of infidelity, betrayal and shadowy hitmen and human traffickers who may not be that they seem.

HEAD TO EILEENORMSBY.COM FOR BUYING OPTIONS

STALKERS

TRUE TALES OF DEADLY OBSESSIONS

Deluded narcissists. Obsessed fans. Sinister internet trolls. Stalkers who turned deadly

A Hollywood starlet on a smash-hit sitcom enjoys rising fame, unaware that her greatest fan is hell-bent on meeting his crush. When she films a love scene, his adoration turns into a quest to see her punished

A gameshow winner turns to writing books. When one is given a scathing review, he tracks down the reviewer with bloody results

A teenage boy enjoys online chatrooms. When he meets a sexy Secret Service operative, she convinces him he has been chosen to be a spy with a licence to kill... and his first target is his own best friend.

Men keep turning up at a newlywed's home convinced that she has placed a Craigslist ad for a rough fantasy roleplay. Things turn violent before police are able to unravel a twisted and diabolical scheme

STALKERS takes you into the twisted world of cyberstalking, catfishing, rejected suitors, jealous exes and celebrity stalkers, and the devastating impact their obsessions can have on their victims. This is a standalone book in the Dark Webs True Crime series. It is not necessary to have read the others in the series

HEAD TO EILEENORMSBY.COM FOR BUYING OPTIONS

LITTLE GIRLS LOST
TRUE TALES OF HEINOUS CRIMES

Four shocking crimes. Four lives lost. Countless lives shattered.

True stories of young lives cut brutally short that will make you want to hug your daughter and never let her go.

⚠ **Note: this is a true crime book that contains descriptions of sexual violence against children. Reader discretion is advised**

An 11-year-old girl never makes it home from a Halloween party. When the people of the tight-knit Oil City discover what was done to her, they cancel Halloween until the real monsters who roam their streets can be caught.

A 14-year-old girl is excited to attend her first evening party with local teens. What happens there is every parent's nightmare, but it is made infinitely worse when the residents of the town close ranks around the perpetrators.

A schoolgirl comes to the aid of a middle-aged woman who has lost her puppy and becomes the victim of the most hated couple in Australian history.

Police tell gang members a 16-year-old girl has agreed to testify against them, with predictable results. When they make an arrest for her murder, a Hollywood sitcom plays a surprising role in the outcome

HEAD TO EILEENORMSBY.COM FOR BUYING OPTIONS

MISHAP OR MURDER?

TRUE TALES OF MYSTERIOUS DEATHS AND DISAPPEARANCES

It takes just seconds for someone to die. But sometimes years later, questions remain: was it an accident, suicide, or something far more sinister?

An elderly couple having an illicit affair disappear into the bush, their campsite destroyed by fire but their vehicle untouched. At first police wonder if they got lost or eloped, but their investigation soon turns to homicide. Who are the mysterious "Hill People" and does a missing drone hold the key to the mystery?

A skydiver plunges to his death and investigators soon discover his parachute had been tampered with. But with a hundred potential murder weapons and just as many suspects who are used to the adrenaline rush of a high-stakes sport, can anyone uncover who did it?

A young mother heads out for a night on the town to celebrate her new car and never comes home. Her text messages and car tracking system tell a story right up to the moment she disappears, leaving police baffled. Did she disconnect the GPS herself or was someone in the car with her that night?

An entire town is wary of a hard-living local man, and none more so than his battered wife. When he disappears and she starts selling his possessions, nobody cares enough to interfere, until his sister starts asking questions. Did he really leave his wife and four children, or do the local mineshafts hold more secrets than gold?

The latest in the Dark Webs True Crime series takes you through these stories and more cases that stumped police and investigators for years.

Was it Mishap... or Murder?

SMALL TOWNS, DARK SECRETS

SOCIAL MEDIA, REALITY TV AND MURDER IN RURAL AMERICA

Two true tales of small-town murders

Unfriendly: How a social media feud led to a double homicide

When a young couple is discovered slain in their home, investigators are drawn into a vicious online feud that had been simmering for over a year. Soon they are drawn into an unbelievable case involving a CIA agent, a secret relationship, and an impressionable local man who had never had a girlfriend. At the center of the chaos was the Potter family: Buddy, Barbara, and their daughter, Jenelle.

Could something as simple as unfriending someone on Facebook really lead to a double homicide?

A Bluegrass Tragedy: The "Wife Swap" murders

The Stockdale Family was private and insular, the children homeschooled, their only outlet playing in the family Bluegrass band. The internet and television were banned, movies and radio programs vetted to ensure they adhered to the family's fundamentalist Christian values.

They kept to themselves on their farm in Ohio, until an unexpected call from the producers of reality TV series Wife Swap upended their world. Was it the scrutiny of a skeptical public that led to the tragic double homicide?

Mountain City, Tennessee and Bolivar, Ohio: just two small towns that harbored dark secrets... and murder

HEAD TO EILEENORMSBY.COM FOR BUYING OPTIONS

SILK ROAD

It was the 'eBay of drugs', a billion dollar empire. Behind it was the
FBI's Most Wanted Man, a mysterious crime czar dubbed 'Dread
Pirate Roberts'. SILK ROAD lay at the heart of the 'Dark Web' - a
parallel internet of porn, guns, assassins and drugs. Lots of drugs.
With the click of a button LSD, heroin, meth, coke, any illegal drug
imaginable, would wing its way by regular post from any dealer to
any user in the world. How was this online drug cartel even
possible? And who was the mastermind all its low roads led to?
This is the incredible true story of Silk Road's rise and fall, told
with unparalleled insight into the main players - including alleged
founder and kingpin Dread Pirate Roberts himself - by lawyer and
investigative journalist Eileen Ormsby. A stunning crime story
with a truth that explodes off the page.

Published by Pan MacMillan

HEAD TO EILEENORMSBY.COM FOR BUYING OPTIONS

FROM THE AUTHOR

Thank you for giving me your valuable time to share these stories with you.

A great deal of work goes into researching these crimes and writing about them in a way that gives voice to the victims. The most important part of how well a book sells is how many positive reviews it has, so if you leave me one then you are directly helping me to continue to report on these stories for you.

Just a line or two is all it takes to make an author's day.

SEARCH FOR "PSYCHO.COM" ON AMAZON OR GOODREADS TO LEAVE YOUR REVIEW

Thank you so much.

REFERENCES

In researching these three stories, as well as court records, transcripts and statements, I consulted hundreds of articles and news reports, many of them translated from Russian, Ukrainian and Portuguese. There are too many items to list individually, but below are some selected pieces

Aamodt, M. G. (2016, September 4). *Serial killer statistics.* Retrieved (October 2019)

Cabrini, Roberto interviews with Pedro Rodrigues Filho for *Connection Reporter* May 2019

Casoy, Ilana, *Serial Killers: Made in Brazil* Darkside Books, 2014

Chilean documentary, *Los maníacos del martillo* (The Hammer Maniacs) 2010

Dewey, Caitlin "Think twice before answering that ad: 101 murders have been linked to Craigslist" in *Washington Post*, January 12 2016

Faustini, Eduardo interview with Pedro Rodrigues Filho for the program *Fantástico* August 1996

Filho, Pedro Rodrigues, *Pedrinho Matador Biografia*, 2019

Kerekes, David, *Killing for Culture - From Edison to ISIS: A New History of Death on Film*

Konova Natalia, Leontyeva Anna, Alexander Ilchenko, Vlad Abramov, "The surviving victim of the Dnieper maniacs is now afraid that the murderers of his friend will not be sent to prison" in *Segodnya* 30 July 2007

Mondonca, Ricardo "A Monster of the System" 2003

Moran, Caitlin "It took 1 min 47 seconds for my memory to become host to a horror that will never go" in *The Times*, January 12 2009

Rezende, Marcelo interviews with Pedro Rodrigues Filho for *Record TV*, 2018

Russian TV news *Killing for Kicks*, 2008

Tetreault, Gilles *The One who Got Away: Escape from the Kill Room*, Canada October 2015

Vronsky, Peter *Serial Killers: The Method and Madness of Monsters* Berkley, 2005